The **FINANCIAL INVESTIGATOR'S** Companion

Further titles available from Police Review Publishing Co:
● **Action Stations: A Guide to OSPRE Part II** ● **Beat Officer's Companion**
● **Scottish Beat Officer's Companion** ● **Traffic Officer's Companion**
● **Custody Officer's Companion** ● **Drug Officer's Companion**
● **PACE – a Guide for the Practitioner** ● **Points to Prove**
● **Summonses and Charges** ● **Taking Statements** ● **Child Protection Manual**
● **Street Survival Skills** ● **Practical Police Management**
● **Special Constable's Manual**
To order or for further details phone 01708 381204 or fax 01708 381211

No part of this publication may be reproduced
or transmitted in any form or by any means, or
stored in any retrieval system of any nature, without prior
written permission, except for permitted fair dealing under
the Copyright, Designs and Patents Act 1988, or in accordance
with the terms of a licence issued by the Copyright Licensing Agency
in respect of photocopying and/or reprographic reproduction.
Application for permission for other use of copyright material
including permission to reproduce extracts in other published works
shall be made to the publishers. Full acknowledgement of
author, publisher and source must be given.

© Geoffrey A Robinson
Michael Badcock   1997

ISBN 0 85164 078 8

**Police Review
Publishing Co**

**Celcon House
289-293, High Holborn
London WC1V 7HU**

Illustrations by Rich King
Typeset by Hairy Toffee Design, Crystal Palace, London SE19
Edited and indexed by Mandy Preece, Bitterne Village, Southampton
Printed and bound in Great Britain by
The Greenacre Press, Northfleet, Kent

Contents

Preface	**v**
Chapter 1 An Overview of the Guide	**1**
Chapter 2 Money Laundering Regulations, Disclosures & Tipping Off in Respect of Disclosures	**17**
Chapter 3 Searches & Social Profiling	**39**
Chapter 4 Production Orders & Warrants	**47**
Chapter 5 Specific Money Laundering Offences	**73**
Chapter 6 Restraint & Charging Orders	**93**
Chapter 7 Confiscation Orders	**107**
Chapter 8 Forfeiture Orders	**129**
Chapter 9 The International Perspective	**137**
Appendix I Sample Production Orders & Warrants	**145**
Appendix II Sample Prosecutor's Statements	**161**
Appendix III The Money Laundering Regulations 1993	**169**
Appendix IV The Drug Trafficking Act 1994, s1	**171**
Index	**173**

Preface

Money laundering is vitally important to drug dealers, fraudsters, terrorists and other criminals. Money is their lifeblood, it is the single common commodity, its powerful lure attracts criminals to their crimes. In order to preserve, increase and carry on their illegal financial activities criminals have, for decades, used and devised ingenious methods of rapidly and safely disposing of financial proceeds and benefits of crime. Money laundering is the generic term which perfectly describes this process. Dirty money, the proceeds or benefit of crime, is first of all placed in the financial system. It is then spun around the system in an effort to hide its source and confuse detection. Once washed the money looses its identity and emerges as clean and legitimate, untainted by its sinister origins.

The United States of America possesses a successful history of combating crime including money laundering through confiscation procedures based in their civil code. It was in the mid-1980s that the United Kingdom's Parliament introduced similar legislation, but rooted it mainly in criminal law. The United Kingdom comprises of three separate jurisdictions, England and Wales, Scotland and Northern Ireland. This guide will primarily refer to England and Wales although both Scotland and Northern Ireland have similar legislation.

The 1986 Drug Trafficking Offences Act was designed to strike at the financial heart of the drug trade by targeting both drug dealer and money launderer. The country's legislators introduced a new Drug Trafficking Act in 1994 and have extended almost identical powers into the crime and terrorist fields, with the 1988 and 1993 Criminal Justice Acts (as amended by the Proceeds of Crime Act 1995), and the Prevention of Terrorism (Temporary Provisions) Act 1989 (as amended by the Criminal Justice Act 1993 and the Criminal Justice and Public Order Act 1994). Other legislation enhances the provisions of these main statutes providing a real weapon against crime and the criminal.

Similar world-wide legislation is growing thanks to mutual legal assistance stimulated by the international resolve to combat the global illicit drug trade and the money-laundering activities of international criminals.

This book has been designed as a practical pocket guide for financial investigators primarily working in England and Wales, in the criminal areas of drugs, crime and terrorism. It does not pretend to contain every section from the relevant legislation but it does refer to the main armoury at the disposal of the financial investigator. Blank pages have been left at the end of the book for making notes about new stated cases or other relevant information.

We have approached the writing of this guide pragmatically and sincerely hope that it will be of great use to all financial investigators from whatever agency. We believe that the concept of financial investigations is the key in the battle against crime and criminals.

Geoffrey A Robinson BSc
Michael Badcock MAAT

Chapter 1
An Overview of the Guide

Chapter 1
An Overview of the Guide

'The theory underlying confiscation is that it relieves the criminal of financial gain from unacceptable social behaviour', so stated Michael Levi and Lisa Osofsky in *Investigating, Seizing and Confiscating the Proceeds of Crime*. This simple statement goes to the heart of the financial investigator's task and it also points at the philosophy behind the concept of confiscation. Before we examine how the investigator can relieve the criminal of financial gain it is important to examine key areas of the development of confiscation as a potential criminal deterrent.

In Britain the philosophy of confiscation is historically rooted in forfeiture which can be traced back to medieval times when a felon convicted of treason forfeited his entire estate as well as being executed. The forfeited wares, going to either the Crown or the feudal Lord, provided those people with a valuable revenue. As time went on forfeiture gradually lost its effectiveness, and the 1870 Forfeiture Act abolished the Crown's prerogative right to the proceeds of forfeiture. Parliament has subsequently re-introduced forfeiture into several statutes, however it refers to actual articles used in the crime and not the proceeds or benefit of crime. For example, under s5 of the Protection of Children Act 1978, a Justice may order forfeiture of any articles seized under s4 of the same Act, those articles could be indecent photographs or pseudo-photographs of children.

Confiscation, in the United Kingdom, as a contemporary judicial power has its conception in a failed attempt to have a drug trafficker's profits forfeited under s27 of the Misuse of Drugs Act 1971. (*R v Cuthbertson* (1981).) In this case it was argued, by the Crown, that the assets of Cuthbertson and others represented the proceeds of supplying Class A drugs and therefore the defendants were ordered to forfeit a monetary sum equal to their total assets. This effectively stretched the definition of forfeiture into the realm of confiscation. Cuthbertson's lawyers objected to this ruling and took their submission to the House of Lords where they successfully submitted that s27 could only apply to the forfeiture of assets and monies actually used in the commission of offences they were convicted of and not the monetary sum equal to their total assets. The Law Lords' hands were tied and they reluctantly ordered the discharge of the forfeiture orders against Cuthbertson and his associates.

This predicament over Cuthbertson led to the 1984 Hodgson Committee report on 'The Profits of Crime and their Recovery' (Heinemann, 1984), which recommended that the criminal courts be able to confiscate the benefit accumulated by the defendant as a direct result of the offence they were convicted of.

Running parallel with the UK's concern over the benefit of crime and the City of London's determination to protect the confidence in its important financial markets, was an international determination to thwart the activities of criminals using national and international financial institutions to launder their money. During the last two decades both the United Nations and European Union have held conferences and have passed resolutions to combat drug trafficking and money laundering by economic means, namely the 1988 UN Convention, 1990 Recommendations of the Financial Action Task Force, 1990 Council of European Convention and the 1991 European Communities Directive. The United States of America, enacted the world's first law making money laundering itself a specific crime, this was the Money Laundering Control Act of 1986.

The importance of investigating organised crime through the financial affairs of its perpetrators has a long pedigree. For the reader who wishes to acquaint themselves with the complicated world-wide evolution of money laundering counter-measures we recommend, *Dirty Money*, by William C. Gilmore and *International Guide to Money Laundering Law and Practice*, edited by Richard Parlour.

Money laundering is the process by which criminals conceal the true origin of the proceeds of their criminal activities. The actual laundering maybe carried out personally by the criminal or some other associate who is aware that they are assisting in this process. In England and Wales Regulation 2(3) of the Money Laundering Regulations 1993 sets out all the offences which constitute 'money laundering' *(see Chapter 2)*. Those regulations

Chapter 1 – An Overview of the Guide

also place responsibilities on persons conducting financial business in order to prevent and detect money-laundering activity. The analogy of comparing the washing of dirty clothes with that of illicitly-obtained money, the laundering process, seems to have been first coined in the early 1970's in the United States of America during the infamous Watergate investigation. During this inquiry it was discovered that confederates of President Nixon laundered cash donations given as donations for a presidential election campaign.

Within the financial investigation fraternity world-wide, it is accepted that the laundering process is achieved in three distinct stages, namely, 'placement or immersion', 'layering' and 'integration'.

Placement or immersion is the act or acts of introducing the illicitly-gained monies into the financial system or purchasing an asset. Layering is disguising the illicit proceeds from their source by creating complex layers of financial transactions in order to camouflage their origins and frustrate detection. Integration is the point were the criminally-derived wealth is brought back in circulation, now in a legitimate form, untainted from its evil origins. These three steps in laundering money may occur simultaneously or they may be separate events of varying length, usually dependant on the availability of safe laundering facilities.

In 1986, the UK's Parliament reacted to domestic and international concern over the illicit drugs trade by enacting the Drug Trafficking Offences Act 1986 which came into force on 12th January 1987. This Act, applicable in England and Wales, gave extensive powers to investigate, preserve and then post-conviction, confiscate a drug trafficker's assets. Major amendments to this Act were contained in the Criminal Justice Act 1993, Part II. In order to clarify drug-trafficking legislation a new Act was passed on 3rd February 1995, the Drug Trafficking Act 1994. It is important to note that the confiscation provisions in the Criminal Justice Act 1993, apply where a person has been charged with a drug-trafficking offence before 3rd February 1995. This guide sets out drug trafficking financial investigation law, mainly for England and Wales, as expressed in the Drug Trafficking Act 1994. All of Scotland's confiscation legislation is contained in the Proceeds of Crime (Scotland) Act 1995.

Northern Ireland uses the Proceeds of Crime (Northern Ireland) Order 1996.

The schematic overview of the Drug Trafficking Act 1994, *see page 13*, may assist the reader to quickly find a relevant section.

The 1986 Fraud Trials Committee chaired by Lord Roskill and public opinion stimulated Parliament to introduce similar drug-trafficking legislation into the field of crime. This manifested itself in Part VI of the Criminal Justice Act 1988, which came into force on the 3rd April 1989 and applied to the proceeds of all indictable offences and some lucrative summary offences. That Act has been subsequently amended by the Criminal Justice Act 1993 (Part III) and the Proceeds of Crime Act 1995, which both apply to England and Wales. Scotland's crime confiscation legislation is contained in the Proceeds of Crime (Scotland) Act 1995, and Northern Ireland's in the Proceeds of Crime (Northern Ireland) Order 1996.

The schematic overview of the Criminal Justice Act 1988 (as amended), *see page 14*, may assist the reader to quickly find a relevant section.

Powers to financially investigate terrorism in the UK was first granted by the Prevention of Terrorism (Temporary Provisions) Act 1989 (Part III), which was amended by the Criminal Justice Act 1993 (Part IV) and the Criminal Justice and Public Order Act 1994. The schematic overview of the Prevention of Terrorism (Temporary Provisions) Act 1989 (as amended), *see page 15*, may assist the reader to quickly find a relevant section.

The schematic overviews, which can be located at the end of this chapter, provide a visual index of the three main pieces of legislation, however, we recommend that reference is also made to the relevant chapter of this guide by using the main index at the rear of the book. Reference to the actual Act or contemporary stated case may also have to be made.

It is also useful to be aware that existing financial legislation has evolved through a number of, now repealed, statutes. We are not going to adjust this guide to cope with the very few pipe-line cases there might be, as this would in our opinion lead to unnecessary complication.

Chapter 1 – An Overview of the Guide

'Money is not only at the root of the problem, it is also at the root of the solution', philosophically stated by Jeffrey Robinson in his book entitled, *The Laundrymen*. World-wide investigating agencies are using money-laundering legislation not just as a reactive opportunity of confiscating proceeds and benefit of crime, but also as a proactive tool in intelligence-led policing.

Intelligence has always been an important part in the police armoury, however contemporary policing is emphasising the importance of an efficiently managed, streamlined intelligence gathering, storage and dissemination system. In fact the majority of police forces in the UK and many foreign police forces are now allowing intelligence to lead them operationally and dominate their objectives and strategies. A flexible, multi-agency, proactive intelligence-gathering network leads to less bureaucracy and improved performance. In the crime arena, it is accepted by police that a few criminals are responsible for the majority of crimes in any one area, therefore by focusing on these criminals police or the relevant agency can arrest and/or disrupt their criminal activities or organisation.

The proactive social or financial profiling of criminals of all levels is a vital tool in intelligence-led policing, such profiling cannot be fully achieved without a financial analysis of the individual in question. Details on how to achieve this financial profile can be found in Chapter 3. The job of compiling such a financial profile is of a specialist nature demanding tenacious and analytic investigative skills. The financial investigator needs to think like the money launderer, constantly reviewing lines of inquiry in an effort to discover the whereabouts of laundered money. The launderer and international fraudsperson is a highly ingenious and resourceful character, the investigator has to be equally ingenious and resourceful.

As well as leading to improved performance intelligence-led policing can help crime prevention through more focused partnership initiatives. Partnership with the local authority, community organisations and commerce is working in many cities and towns in the UK. Another form of crime prevention is the rehabilitation of offenders, 'if criminals are convinced that "crime does not pay," and that (if caught) they will be unable to retain their ill-gotten gains, then, presumably, at least some criminals will be deterred from committing crimes', according to

Levi and Osofsky.[1] If this common sense observation is correct then financial investigations should occupy a higher profile in core policing activities and training at all levels, a recommendation that both Levi and Osofsky make throughout their research.

Suspicion and Reasonable Grounds to Suspect

Before we move into the main body of the guide, which will equip the investigator with the law and procedures necessary to conduct a financial investigation, let us briefly examine the concepts of 'suspicion' and 'reasonable grounds to suspect'. These concepts crop up throughout all the legislation concerning the investigation and confiscation of laundered money.

In *Baker v Oxford* (1980), the Divisional Court accepted that there was a difference between 'believe' and 'suspect', but did not clarify what the distinction was. It was proposed that 'suspect' implied an imagination that something exists without proof, 'believe' implied an acceptance of what was true. Suspicion therefore is based on the subjectivity which was supported by Lord Devlin in *Hussien v Chong Fook Kam* (1970), 'suspicion is a state of conjecture or surmise where proof is lacking'. 'If, therefore, there are ten steps from mere suspicion to a state of certainty, or an acceptance that something is true, then reasonable suspicion may be as low as step two or three, whilst reasonable belief may be as high as step nine or ten'.[2]

Castorina v Chief Constable of Surrey (1988), *Siddiqui v Swain* (1979), both comment on the words 'has reasonable cause to suspect' in respect of arrest. A constable's suspicion, in the context of an arrest, may arise from information he has received or from what he has personally seen or heard. This is more than just the officer's assertion, there must be some element of objectivity to the constable's subjective, 'reasonable cause to suspect'. Consequently, if there was no reasonable basis upon which a constable based his subjective suspicions, then a judge and/or jury could draw the conclusion that he had no such suspicion. (*DPP v Morgan* (1976), and *R v Williams* (1984).)

---

[1] 'Investigating, Seizing and Confiscating the Proceeds of Crime' by Michael Levi and Lisa Osofsky.

[2] 'The Investigation of Crime – A Guide to Police Powers' by Vaughan Bevan and Ken Lidstone.

Chapter 1 – An Overview of the Guide

In order to arrive at whether there is suspicion or reasonable grounds to suspect, the person making that decision is not constrained, as is the court, by rules of evidence. Whether making a decision to arrest, disclose or apply for an order under money laundering and confiscation legislation the person may draw on information from any source but must always be ready to satisfy their grounds for suspicion or reasonable grounds to suspect. Anonymous information would not on its own constitute reasonable grounds to suspect, however if the information could be verified, supported or corroborated the person may form the opinion that they have reasonable grounds to suspect. *Isaacs v Brand* (1817) suggests that information from an accomplice in a crime cannot be the basis of reasonable cause to suspect or for that matter reasonable cause to believe. Such a decision taken in the early eighteenth century may very well be successfully counter argued with a suitable contemporary case. We await with interest such a case.

A constable acting on information supplied by a colleague may be justified in acting on it without verification, however, if challenged, the colleague's information must be able to be called upon and examined.

Code A of the Police and Criminal Evidence Act 1984 refers to the Code of Practice for the Exercise by Police Officers of Statutory Powers of Stop and Search, also assists us in our quest to define suspicion or reasonable grounds to suspect. Paragraph 1.6 states, 'Whether a reasonable ground for suspicion exists will depend on the circumstances in each case, but there must be some objective basis for it', clearly supporting the above reasoning.

Chapter Overviews
Chapter 2 – Money Laundering Regulations, Disclosures & 'Tipping Off' in Respect of Disclosures
The duty to disclose suspicious financial transactions primarily lies in s52 of the Drug Trafficking Act 1994, s93A of the Criminal Justice Act 1988 (as amended) and s18 of the Prevention of Terrorism (Temporary Provisions) Act 1989. As well as examining these sections, Chapter 2 refers to the Money Laundering Regulations 1993 (MLR 93), which came into force on 1st April 1994. These Regulations set up the legal framework for financial institutions to legally breach their duty of confidentiality

and disclose transactions they suspect may be money-laundering activities. The regulations define who an *applicant for business* is; what a *money laundering* offence is; what *criminal conduct, business relationship, relevant financial business* are; and what is *not relevant financial business*. The regulations also set out, *systems for training staff* to prevent money laundering and indicate a *defence clause* and *corporate responsibility*, which extends the offence to companies, partnerships, and members, where they have connived, or consented, or are attributable to neglect in respect of laundering.

The Regulations also clearly set out *identification procedures*, which must be adhered to by staff dealing with clients or potential clients who wish to enter into some sort of fiscal business with the institution. Importantly, the Regulations clearly set out *Disclosure Requirements and Procedures*, for the relevant financial institution. Disclosure within the context of these Regulations and the primary legislation referred to at the beginning of this chapter's overview on *page 9*, is the passing on of confidential information obtained by the financial institution to a constable. A constable within the meaning of these regulations in practice is the National Criminal Intelligence Service (NCIS).

A flowchart in the chapter explains how a disclosure can be dealt with by a Supervisory Authority, person or Inspector appointed under the MLR 93. The Supervisory Authority, person or Inspector being defined later in the chapter. A number of financial institutions have appointed an individual, known as 'the money laundering reporting officer', through whom all disclosures are routed and all inquiries under money-laundering legislation is passed. Regulation 14 specifically states that an appropriate person has to be appointed.

The UK therefore has a suspicion-based disclosure system, reliant on the subjective decision of an individual. Interestingly the disclosure system in the USA is based on an automatic reporting system, all financial transactions of $10,000 or over being forwarded to the US Treasury Department. We do not propose to enter into the already raging debate over the merits of one system over another. In our opinion both systems can be circumvented by an astute and knowledgeable launderer. It is important for those charged with identifying dubious transactions, in whatever system, to be vigilant and aware that it

Chapter 1 – An Overview of the Guide

is not unknown for criminals to infiltrate organisations either directly or through corruption.

As well as commenting on disclosure, Chapter 2 also looks at the concept of 'Tipping Off', this being the telling of information to any person which prejudices a disclosure, an investigation or proposed investigation into such a disclosure.

Chapter 3 – Searches & Social Profiling
Examines the actual investigative process common to all inquiries and suggests how a social profile, financially based, can greatly assist in deciding the future action to be taken against sophisticated and hamfisted criminals alike. The concept of 'unused material' and the implications of the Criminal Procedure and Investigations Act 1996 is reviewed. The basic theory of underground banking is also examined.

Chapter 4 – Production Orders & Warrants
Needs very little further explanation as schematic diagrams clearly outline the law and requirements for obtaining such orders and warrants under the Criminal Justice Act 1988 (as amended), Drug Trafficking Act 1994, Prevention of Terrorism (Temporary Provisions) Act 1989 and Police and Criminal Evidence Act 1984 to carry out financial investigations.

Chapter 5 – Specific Money Laundering Offences
Examines the specific money laundering offences created to cover: assisting in retaining benefit; acquisition, possession or use of the direct or indirect proceeds; and concealing or transferring of the direct or indirect proceeds in respect of crime and drug trafficking. The seizure and detention of cash being either imported or exported from the UK is explored. The offence of 'Tipping Off' parties that a constable is conducting an investigation into money laundering or a disclosure is also reviewed. Financial assistance for terrorism; obtaining contributions to resources of proscribed organisations; assisting in retention or control of funds; and disclosure of information, all under the Prevention of Terrorism (Temporary Provisions) Act 1989 are also examined.

Chapter 6 – Restraint & Charging Orders
Examines restraint in respect of drugs, crime and terrorism and charging orders with reference to drugs and crime.

Chapter 7 – Confiscation Orders
Looks at confiscation procedures for crime and drug offences. It examines the concepts of postponed determination, assumptions, prosecutor's statement and the review and revision of confiscation orders.

Chapter 8 – Forfeiture Orders
Examines the concept of forfeiture in respect of drugs, crime and terrorism and explains how property can be forfeited.

Chapter 9 – The International Perspective
Briefly summarises the history of the international resolve to combat the illicit drug trade, money laundering and crime. The chapter also gives practical information for the financial investigator working in the UK.

Appendix 1
Includes sample informations, production orders and warrants under the Drug Trafficking Act 1994 and Criminal Justice Act 1988.

Appendix 2
Is a sample 'prosecutor's statement' under both the Drug Trafficking Act 1994 and Criminal Justice Act 1988.

Appendix 3
Shows the Money Laundering Regulations 1993.

Note: Use the blank pages at the back of this book to customise and update your guide. Keep an eye on the law reports in the broad-sheet newspapers for relevant cases, and read appropriate articles in police magazines, such as Police Review.

Chapter 1 – An Overview of the Guide

An Overview of the Drug Trafficking Act 1994
(main sections)

---

s1 – defines drug trafficking & drug trafficking offence
s2 – confiscation orders
s3 – postponed determination
s4 – assessing proceeds
s5 – amount to be recovered
s6 – meaning of 'amount'
s7 – value of property
s8 – gifts
s9 – fines
s10 – interest
s11 – prosecutor's statement
s12 – information by defendant
s13 – reconsideration
s14 – re-assessment
s15 – revised assessment
s16 – increase in realisable property
s17 – inadequacy of realisable property
s18 – compensation
s19 – defendant dead or absconded
s25-26 – restraint orders
s27-28 – charging orders
s53 – disclosure & money laundering regs. 1993
s55 – production order
s56 – search warrant

Offences in connection with the proceeds of drug trafficking
s42 – seizure & detention of money imported or exported
s43 – forfeiture
s49 – concealing
s50 – assisting another
s51 – acquisition
s52 – failure to disclose
s53 – tipping off
s58 – prejudicing an investigation
s59 – disclosure of information held by government depts

An Overview of the Criminal Justice Act 1988
As amended by the Criminal Justice Act 1993 & Proceeds of Crime Act 1995 (main sections)

References in brackets refer to the amending legislation
ie PCA = Proceeds of Crime Act   CJA 93 = Criminal Justice Act 1993

---

s93A – Assisting another to retain benefit
(s29 CJA 93)

s93B – Acquisition, possession or use of proceeds
(s30 CJA 93)

s93C – Concealing, transferring proceeds
(s31 CJA 93)

s93D – Tipping off
(s32 CJA 93)

s93E – Application of 93A to 93D to Scotland
(s33 CJA 93)

s93F – Prosecution by Customs & Excise
(s35 CJA 93)

---

s71 – Duty to make confiscation order
(s1 PCA)

s72 – Confiscation & assumptions
(s2 PCA)

s73 – Prosecutor's statement
(s3 PCA)

s73A – Provision of information by defendant
(s4 PCA)

s75 – Enforcement of confiscation order
(s8 PCA)

---

s96 & s97 – Enforcement of external confiscation order

---

s93H – Production order
(s11 PCA)

---

s12 – Search warrant
(s12 PCA)

---

s13 – Disclosure of information by government dept.

---

s76 & s77 – Restraint
(s8 PCA)
s78 – Charging order

---

s74A – Review of cases where proceeds of crime not assessed
(s5 PCA)

s74B – Revision of assessment of proceeds of crime
(s6 PCA)

s74C – Revision of assessment of amount to be recovered
(s7 PCA)

s75A – Interest on sums unpaid under confiscation orders
(s9 PCA)

s80 to s83 – Realisation of property and other matters concerned with the receiver
(s8 & s10 PCA)

Chapter 1 – An Overview of the Guide

An Overview of the Prevention of Terrorism (Temporary Provisions) Act 1989 (Part III & Schedule 7) As amended by Criminal Justice Act 1993 (Part IV) & Criminal Justice and Public Order Act 1994 (Part VI) (main sections)

References in brackets refer to the amending legislation
ie CJA 93 = Criminal Justice Act 1993
CJPO 94 = Criminal Justice & Public Order Act 1994

---

s9 – contributions towards acts of terrorism
(s49(1) CJA 93)
s10 – contributions to resources of proscribed organisations
(s49(2) CJA 93)
s11 – assisting in retention or control of terrorist funds
s12 – disclosure of information about terrorist funds
(s49 (3) to (6) CJA 93)
s13 – penalties & forfeiture
Schedule 4 – forfeiture, restraint, compensation & enforcement

s17(1) – defines terrorist investigations
(s50 CJA 93)
s17(2) – tipping off
(s50 (3) to (9) CJA 93)
s18 – information about acts of terrorism
s18A failure to disclose knowledge or suspicion of offences under s9 or s11
(s51 CJA 93)
s19 – prosecutions & evidence
s20 – definitions including 'terrorism'

Schedule 7 Part 1
Para 1 – interpretations
Para 2 – warrant to search for items not subject of legal privilege
Para 3 – production order for excluded or special procedure material
(s83(1)(a) CJPO 94)
Para 4 – provision to vary para 3 above
(s83(1)(b) CJPO 94)
Para 5 – warrant to search for excluded or special procedure material
Para 6 – a judge may order a person to provide an explanation in respect of material seized under paras 2, 3 or 5 above. False or misleading statements can be punished
Para 7 – in urgent cases a police officer of at least the rank of supt can give authority to search as of paras 2 or 5 above
Para 8 – orders by the Secretary of State in relation to certain investigations
(s83(1)(c) CJPO 94)
Para 9 – access to land registry
Para 10 – supplementary

Chapter 2
Money Laundering Regulations, Disclosures & Tipping Off in Respect of Disclosures

Chapter 2
Money Laundering Regulations, Disclosures & Tipping Off in Respect of Disclosures

During the seventeenth century Great Britain, and in particular London, grew as one of the world's greatest trading nations. The nation's sailing vessels plied their trade throughout Europe and started exploring new lands. As a consequence one of the largest financial markets was founded. In 1694 the Bank of England was founded in the City of London and other financial businesses associated with trade and commerce rapidly grew in nearby coffee houses. Such business included dealing in commodities and marine insurance. Notably among the coffee houses were Johnathan's and Lloyd's the latter giving its name to the present day insurance market.

Today London has markets in shares, derivatives, futures, bonds, commodities, insurance, shipping, banking, foreign exchange, pensions, and many more financial businesses not only in London but throughout the UK. Operating in such a varied market internationally, are the world's banks, securities houses, insurance and other financial institutions who have found the need for at least one branch or office within London or the UK. These branches service not only the UK domestic market, but with their unique position within the time zones of the world, services the European, American, African and Asian markets.

This unique position in the world markets makes the United Kingdom an attractive place in which to launder the proceeds of the world's drug money and any other illicitly-gained monies. 'There is no doubt that London plays a major role in money laundering operations, albeit at the end – usually the relatively innocent end of the cycle' (*Organised Crime*, Dr Barry AK Rider). The UK authorities recognised the importance of the commercial world for money launderers and have actively participated in United Nations, European Union and

Commonwealth conferences on the subject of money laundering. They are also a founder member of the Financial Action Task Force (FATF) which in 1990 made 40 recommendations and formed the basis of the present 26 member's money-laundering legislation. England and Wales in fact already had legislative controls in place to regulate various parts of the financial sector, for example the Financial Services Act 1986, Banking Act 1987 and the Companies Act of 1985. This legislation set up the formation of a number of regulatory bodies under the supervision of the Securities and Investment Board who had responsibility for policing the finance and commercial industry.

It is against this background that on 1st April 1994 the Money Laundering Regulations 1993 came into force. This guide will only refer to the Regulations of England and Wales, for Scotland and Northern Ireland you must refer to their respective legislation. It is important to be aware, however, that primary disclosure legislation is contained in s52 of the Drug Trafficking Act 1994, s93A of the Criminal Justice Act 1988 (as amended) and s18 of the Prevention of Terrorism (Temporary Provisions) Act 1989. *See pages 32-38.*

The Money Laundering Regulations 1993

The Regulations require financial institutions to put in place systems to deter money laundering, and assist the relevant authorities to detect money-laundering activities. They were implemented by the UK in response to the FATF recommendations and made by the Treasury under s2(2) of the European Communities Act 1972.

The Regulations specifically exempt business relationships that had commenced prior to the commencement date of these Regulations. This does not absolve business relationships prior to that date from other legislation in force, that is the Drug Trafficking Offences Act 1986 or the Criminal Justice Act 1988. Those Acts had amendments requiring the disclosure of money laundering but had little or no requirement to identify or keep identification of their clients or maintain such material for 5 years until the Money Laundering Regulations came into force.

In total there are 17 Regulations, these are briefly set out in Appendix III. We will now examine and explain the more important regulations.

Chapter 2 – Regulations, Disclosures & Tipping Off

Regulation 2 – Applicant for Business
Sets out interpretations of certain phrases, e.g. 'applicant for business' which means a person seeking to form a business relationship with a person carrying on relevant financial business in the UK.

Regulation 2(3) – Money Laundering
Defines 'money laundering' as any act constituting an offence under the following sections:

- Sections 49, 50 and 51 of the Drug Trafficking Act 1994 relating to handling or assisting in the retention, etc. of the proceeds of drug trafficking.

- Sections 93A, 93B or 93C of the Criminal Justice Act 1988 that relate to the handling, etc. of the proceeds of criminal conduct.

- Section 11 of the Prevention of Terrorism Act 1989 that relate to financial assistance to acts of terrorism relating to Northern Ireland.

- Section 14 of the Criminal Justice (International Co-operation) Act 1990 that relates to concealing or transferring proceeds of drug trafficking beyond the jurisdiction of the UK courts.

- Sections 42A or 43 of the Criminal Justice (Scotland) Act 1987 that relates to handling etc of proceeds of drug trafficking in Scotland.

- Sections 53 or 54 of the Northern Ireland Emergency Provisions Act 1991 that relates to terrorist funding.

- Any provision subsequently made in Northern Ireland that corresponds to any of the above-mentioned offences in England and Wales or Scotland.

The latter paragraph is due to the fact that Northern Ireland is in the process of enacting its own money-laundering legislation.

Regulation 2(7) – Criminal Conduct
Defines 'criminal conduct' as:

- Conduct to which this Act applies (ie set out in Regulation 2(3) above); or

- Conduct which:
  - would constitute an offence in England, Wales or Scotland; and
  - contravenes the law of the country in which it occurred.

Regulation 2(7)(b) would appear an attempt to cover the international aspects of money laundering where the offence originates abroad but crosses the England and Wales jurisdiction by all or part of the money laundering occurring abroad resulting in laundered funds arriving in England or Wales.

Regulation 3 – Business Relationship
Defines a 'business relationship' as an arrangement between two or more persons where one is acting in the course of a business in order to facilitate any payment or transaction on a frequent, habitual or regular basis and the totality of payments to be made is not known or capable of being ascertained at the outset of such business. This means the legislation does not cover 'one off' transactions but see regulation 7(4) where if they amount to more than 15,000 ECU (approximately £12,350 in 1997) evidence of identity is required.

Regulation 4 – Relevant Financial Business
Defines 'relevant financial business' which is briefly:

- All banks, building societies, and other credit institutions.

- All individuals and investment business authorised under the Financial Services Act 1986, generally these are persons and companies licensed to give investment advice either as principles or as Independent Financial Advisors such as lawyers or accountants who give investment advice or as agents of large licensed companies such as stockbrokers.

- All insurance companies and the life business of Lloyd's of London which includes all agents and representatives selling such insurance.

- Other financial activity listed in the Second Banking Supervision Directive including all bureaux de change, money transmission services and licensed deposit takers.

Chapter 2 – Regulations, Disclosures & Tipping Off

Regulation 4 – Not Relevant Financial Business
Also includes a definition of business that is not relevant financial business defined as business carried on under the Industrial and Provident Societies Act 1965, any business of the Bank of England and any business specified under ss45 or 46 of the Financial Services Act 1986 which are businesses specifically exempt from registering under the Act.

Regulation 5(1) – Systems for Training
Sets out the need to implement systems and training to prevent money laundering by stating that no person shall in the course of relevant financial business form a business relationship or carry out a one-off transaction unless that person:

- Maintains the following procedures in relation to that business:
    - identification procedures set out in regulations 7 and 9
    - record keeping procedures set out in regulation 12
    - internal reporting procedures set out in regulation 14
    - such other internal controls as appropriate to prevent money laundering.

- Takes appropriate measures for making employees who handle relevant financial business aware of:
    - the procedures above
    - the enactments relating to money laundering; and

- Provides employees with training in the recognition and handling of transactions which may be carried out by any person engaged in money laundering.

Regulation 5(2) – Penalty
Any person who contravenes these Regulations shall be guilty of an offence and liable on summary conviction to a fine not exceeding the statutory maximum, or upon indictment, to two years' imprisonment and/or a fine.

Regulation 5(4) – Defence Clause
Provides a defence with onus on the person charged to show that all reasonable steps were taken to avoid committing the offence.

Regulation 6 – Corporate Responsibility
Extends the offence in regulation 5(2) to companies, partnerships, and members, where they have connived, or consented, or are attributable to neglect, they shall be proceeded against as if they were a person under regulation 5(2).

Regulation 7(1) – Identification Procedures
Identification procedures are in accordance with the Regulations if they require as soon as is reasonably practicable after business contact is first made:

- The production by the applicant of evidence of identity, or
- The taking of such measures as will produce satisfactory evidence of identity.

If such identity is not obtained then the business relationship shall not proceed any further.

Regulation 11(1) – Satisfactory Identification
Evidence of identity is satisfactory if:

- It is capable of establishing that an applicant is the person claimed to be, and
- The person obtaining evidence of identity is satisfied that it does establish that fact.

Identification Procedures
Responding to the Regulations the banks and building societies use a common rule book, which may provide evidence of best practice, extracts of which have been summarised to be the following.

Account Opening for Personal Customers

1. UK Resident Personal Customers
- The following information should be obtained from prospective UK customers:
  - true name and/or names used
  - correct permanent UK address, including postal code
  - date of birth.

Chapter 2 – Regulations, Disclosures & Tipping Off

- The true name or names used should be verified by reference to documents obtained from a reputable source that bear photographs. Wherever possible a current valid full passport or national identity card should be requested and the details recorded.

  Customers may produce a wide range of documents evidencing their identity, it is for individuals to decide the authenticity of such documents in the light of any other security procedures operated at account opening.

- In addition to the name verification, it is important that the current permanent address should be verified. Some suggested means of verifying the address are:
  - checking the Electoral Roll
  - making a credit reference agency search
  - requesting sight of a recent utility bill, local authority tax bill, bank or building society documents (remember to guard against forged or counterfeit documents, only originals should be accepted)
  - checking a local telephone directory.

- Any introduction from a respected customer personally known to the manager, or from a trusted member of staff, may assist the verification procedure but does not replace the need for address verification set out above. Details of the introduction will be recorded on the customer's file.

- It is acknowledged that there may be exceptional circumstances when persons may not be able to provide documentary evidence of their identity, and where independent address verification is not possible. In such cases a 'manager' in the branch could authorise the opening of an account if satisfied with the circumstances. The manager should record these circumstances in the same manner and for the same period of time as other identification records (5 years under regulation 12).

  When opening accounts for students or other young people, the normal identification procedures set out above should be followed as far as possible. Where such procedures would not be relevant, or do not provide satisfactory evidence of identity, verification could be obtained via the home address of the parent(s) or by inquiries of their school, college or university.

2. Opening Accounts by Post

Any mechanism that avoids face to face contact between banks or building societies and customers poses difficulties for customer identification. Clearly, in such situations, photographic evidence of identity is inappropriate, therefore particular care should be taken when dealing with applications for accounts providing cheque and money transmission facilities which are opened by post, or from coupon applications, to ensure that personal verification and the guidance given above for verification of address has been followed in all respects. In relation to the latter paragraph, regulation 8 also covers this type of business as follows.

3. Postal and Telephone Business – Fixed Term and Fixed Amounts – Regulation 8(1)

Where evidence of identity would, apart from this regulation, be required but:

- The circumstances are such that payment is made by the applicant for business; and

- It is reasonable in the circumstances for the payment to be sent by post, electronic means, or details of such to be given by telephone, electronic means or post.

Then, subject to the fact that the payment is debited from an account held in the applicant's name at an authorised institution, that shall constitute the required evidence of identity. However, a cheque drawn on another bank or building society may only be relied upon where there is no variation between the name on the application form and the name on the cheque. Payments from joint accounts are considered acceptable for this purpose.

The waiver of additional verification requirements for postal transactions covers fixed term, fixed amount, and investment-related products that do not provide money transmission facilities. The waiver does not apply to the following:

- Accounts or investment products that provide cheque or other money transmission facilities.

- Accounts or products where funds can be transferred to other types of accounts which provide cheque or money transmission facilities.

Chapter 2 – Regulations, Disclosures & Tipping Off

- Situations where funds can be repaid or transferred to a person other than the original customer.

Regulation 7(3)
The waiver of additional verification requirements for postal business does not apply where there is any suspicion of money laundering.

Regulation 7(4)
Evidence of identity is required in all business relationships where business is 15,000 ECU (approximately £12,350) or more, or linked transactions that total that amount.

Regulations 9 & 10 – Exemptions from Identity Requirements
Exemptions apply for business transactions where the payment is sent by post or electronic transfer and the transfer is made from an account held in the applicant's name at an institution holding the required identification. In effect this means where any institution holding the required identification wishes to move funds on behalf of the customer to another institution they are exempt from requiring further identity information.

Regulation 12 – Retention of Records
Records of a person's identity obtained for the purpose of this regulation must be stored for a minimum of 5 years after the termination of business.

The records retained must:

- Indicate the nature of evidence obtained.
- Comprise of a copy of the evidence or provide such information to allow the copy of the identity to be obtained.
- Record all transactions carried on in the course of relevant financial business.

Regulation 14 – Central Point of Contact with Law Enforcement Agencies
This requires businesses regulated by this Act to appoint an appropriate person as a contact point for Law Enforcement Agencies. The British Bankers' Association and the National

Criminal Intelligence Service (NCIS) refer to this person as the 'money laundering reporting officer', however, companies registered under the Financial Services Act have a compliance officer and this person will perform the dual role.

Regulation 16 – Disclosure Requirements

The disclosure referred to here is not disclosures by police to third parties, such as the defence solicitors. It is the disclosure of confidential information by third parties to police, relating to suspicious business transactions they have undertaken or are about to undertake. There is no requirement in any legislation for the disclosure of information received in the course of non-business life. Discloseable information must come to the person disclosing in the course of business and be disclosed because of a suspicion that money laundering (regulation 2(3)) is taking place. The Regulations are further complicated by the fact that they refer to groups of persons specified under the Regulations: a supervisory authority under regulation 15(2), supervising persons under regulation 16(6), and a secondary recipient defined under regulation 16(7). In order to understand these disclosure requirements it is necessary to look at the flow chart on the following page, in conjunction with those definitions which are set out here.

Regulation 15(2) – Supervisory Authority

For the purposes of these Regulations, each of the following is a supervisory authority:

- The Bank of England.
- The Building Societies Commission.
- A designated agency within the meaning of the Financial Services Act 1986:
  - the Secretary of State has designated the Securities and Investments Board (SIB).
- A recognised self-regulating organisation within the meaning of the Financial Services Act 1986; a body which regulates the investment business such as Personal Investment Authority (PIA), Investment Management Regulatory Organisation (IMRO), Life Assurance & Unit Trust Regulatory Organisation (LAUTRO) and the Securities & Futures Authority (SFA). *(continued overleaf, page 30)*

Chapter 2 – Regulations, Disclosures & Tipping Off

Money Laundering Regulations 1993 Disclosure Requirements

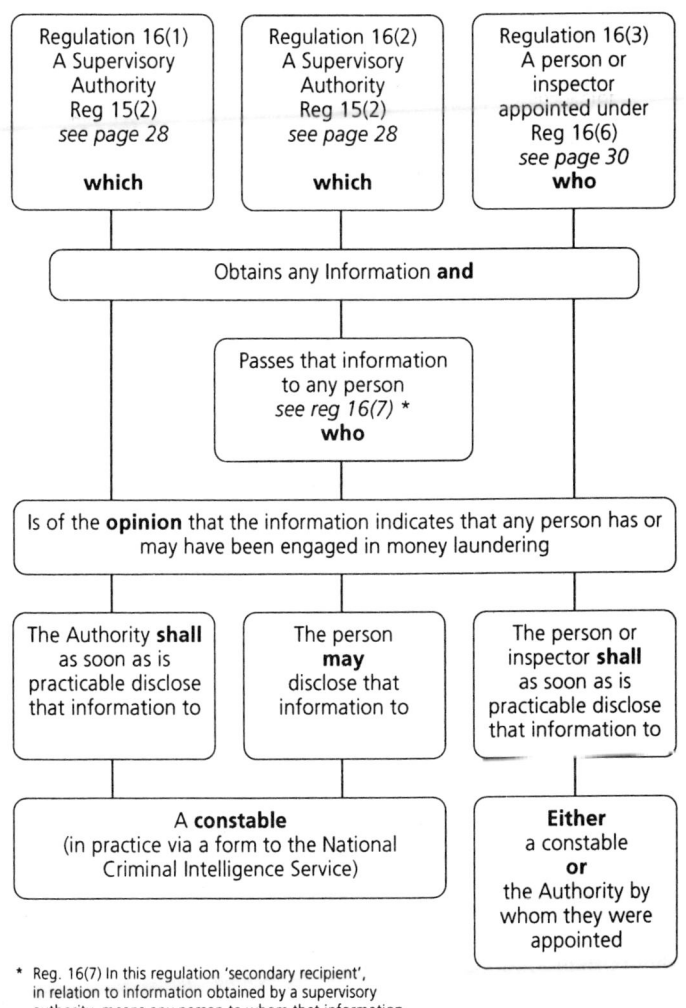

* Reg. 16(7) In this regulation 'secondary recipient', in relation to information obtained by a supervisory authority, means any person to whom that information has been passed by the authority.

(continued from page 28)

- A recognised professional body within the meaning of the Financial Services Act 1986; eg Law Society, Chartered Association of Certified Accountants (ACCA), Institute of Actuaries and many more.
- A transferee body within the meaning of the Financial Services Act 1986; the Friendly Societies Commission have transferred certain responsibilities to the Securities and Investments Board (SIB).
- A recognised self-regulating organisation for friendly societies within the meaning of the Financial Services Act 1986; in this case the Personal Investment Authority (PIA).
- The Secretary of State.
- The Treasury.
- The Council of Lloyd's.
- The Director General of Fair Trading.
- The Friendly Societies Commission.
- The Chief Registrar of Friendly Societies.
- The Central Office of the Registry of Friendly Societies.
- The Registrar of Friendly Societies for Northern Ireland.
- The Assistant Registrar of Friendly Societies for Scotland.

Regulation 15(3)

These Regulations apply to the Secretary of State in the exercise, in relation to any person carrying on relevant financial business, of his functions under the enactments relating to insurance companies, companies or insolvency or under the Financial Services Act 1986.

Regulation 16(6) – Supervising Persons / Inspectors

The types of person or inspectors shown in regulation 16(6) are the type of persons who could be employed to examine or audit companies for or on behalf of the Supervisory Authorities in regulation 15(2). It is only right that they should be able to report their findings to the instructing body who should then decide whether to disclose the information to the police or may report direct to the police if they consider it right to do so.

Chapter 2 – Regulations, Disclosures & Tipping Off

Persons falling within this paragraph are:

- A person or inspector appointed under s17 of the Industrial Assurance Act 1923 or ss65 or 66 of the Friendly Societies Act 1992.
- An inspector appointed under s49 of the Industrial and Provident Societies Act 1965 or s18 of the Credit Unions Act 1979.
- An inspector appointed under ss431, 432, 442 or 446 of the Companies Act 1985 or under articles 424, 425, 435 or 439 of the Companies (Northern Ireland) Order 1986.
- A person or inspector appointed under ss55 or 56 of the Building Societies Act 1986.
- An inspector appointed under ss94 or 177 of the Financial Services Act 1986.
- A person appointed under s41 of the Banking Act 1987.
- A person authorised to require the production of documents under s44 of the Insurance Companies Act 1982, s447 of the Companies Act 1985, s106 of the Financial Services Act 1986, article 440 of the Companies (Northern Ireland) Order 1986, or s84 of the Companies Act 1989.

Regulation 16(4) – Legal Protection for Disclosure

Any disclosure made by virtue of these Regulations shall not be treated as a breach of any restriction imposed by statute or otherwise.

This regulation protects the disclosing party from any action for breach of any civil, criminal or common law imposed contract of confidentiality.

Regulation 16(5) – Information Received by Police

Any information disclosed to a constable under the Regulations may be disclosed, by the constable or any person obtaining the information directly or indirectly from the constable, in connection with the investigation of any criminal offence or for purpose of any criminal proceedings but not otherwise.

This regulation has the effect of allowing police officers to pursue any disclosure by telling other persons the content, in order to illicit further information, but it must be in connection with the investigation of a criminal offence or process of criminal proceedings. This may contradict the ruling in *Marcel v Metropolitan Police Commissioner* (1991) where police had a duty of confidentiality of information obtained by the service of a production order under PACE 1984 and could not pass that information without a court order. This section was not in force and in any event relates to information disclosed to police and not obtained by virtue of a court order. The regulation is required as it would be impossible in most cases to investigate a disclosure without asking other parties involved in the transaction about the matters set out in the disclosure.

There is, however, a need to temper the inquiries with a degree of caution. Recently a bank disclosed information on their customer, a solicitor, who had made use of various credit cards in Holland and Indonesia, and had excessive turnover of cash transactions for a salaried person. The officer dealing with the disclosure made a confidential inquiry of the solicitor's employer, however the employer later broke that confidence and approached the solicitor demanding an explanation. The upshot of this case was that the bank apologised to the customer and paid out compensation. Here it is difficult to see what action could have been taken to prevent these circumstances save for the bank to run a risk of prosecution for failing to disclose.

This regulation does not absolve officers from the need to obtain a production order to elicit information from a party who holds it in confidence and does not wish to discuss information without such an order, it merely allows an officer to pass what would otherwise be confidential information in the hands of police in order to progress the inquiry. This is an important area which could as a result of abuse be withdrawn in the future, confidential information should be treated as such and never passed on without considering the need for such action within the realms of this legislation.

Disclosures Under Other Acts

Section 52 Drug Trafficking Act 1994

Points to Prove
- The suspicion is that a person is engaged in drug money laundering (ss49, 50, or 51 offences).

Chapter 2 – Regulations, Disclosures & Tipping Off

- That the information on which the suspicion is based came into being in the course of a trade, business, profession or employment.
- That the information was not disclosed as soon as practicable to a relevant person or a constable.
- That the information was not the subject of claims of legal privilege or if it came about in the course of privileged legal consultation then it was in furtherance of a criminal enterprise.

Maximum Penalty
On conviction on indictment, 5 years' imprisonment, a fine or both; summarily, 6 months' imprisonment or the statutory maximum fine or both. (See Chapter 1 for an explanation of 'suspicion'.)

Section 18 Prevention of Terrorism (Temporary Provisions) Act 1989

Points to Prove
- The person has information which he knows or believes to be of material assistance:
  - in preventing the commission by any person of an act of terrorism connected with Northern Ireland
  - in securing the apprehension, prosecution or conviction of any other person for an offence involving preparation or instigation of terrorism.
- The person failed to disclose that information in England, or Wales, to a constable, in Northern Ireland to a constable or member of HM forces, or in Scotland to a constable or procurator fiscal.

Maximum Penalty
On conviction on indictment, 5 years' imprisonment, a fine or both; summarily, 6 months' imprisonment, statutory fine or both.

Defence
The Drug Trafficking Act 1994, the Criminal Justice Act 1988 (as amended), and the Prevention of Terrorism (Temporary Provisions) Act 1989 all provide a defence to a prosecution of failing to disclose money laundering as follows:

- That the person charged had a reasonable excuse for not disclosing suspicions of money laundering.
- That the person charged was a professional legal advisor and the information came to their attention in the course of privileged circumstances and not in pursuance of a course of criminal conduct. (Legal privilege is defined within the Acts as per s10(1) of the Police and Criminal Evidence Act 1984, *see page 52.*)
- That the person charged had disclosed the information to a constable or an appropriate person in accordance with procedures established within their employment.
- That the person charged intended to disclose to a constable as soon as possible after the action concerned.
- That the person charged did the act on his or her own initiative and then disclosed the act as soon as it was reasonable to do so thereafter.
- The person charged had disclosed the information prior to the act and a constable consented to the action.

The Acts also provide that where a person discloses to a constable or any other person the suspicion or belief that a person is concerned in money laundering, the disclosure shall not be in breach of any restriction by statute or otherwise not to disclose such information. This paragraph has the effect of releasing the person from either their civil, criminal, or common law agreement of confidentiality providing they have acted within the relevant legislation and had the reasonable belief money laundering was taking place. In all of the Acts the suspicion of money laundering and the decision whether to disclose must be that of the person disclosing. Police officers cannot pass on suspicion to another but another person may be persuaded to look at their information in a different light and then disclose that information.

It can be seen that there is no requirement in legislation under any of the Acts on persons who come across information other than in the course of business to disclose that information to anyone. The person for instance who is unemployed and hears two people in a public house discussing the movement of laundered drug money would have no requirement under this legislation to disclose that to anyone but may under common law have a duty to assist the police.

In conclusion then, specified persons are controlled by the Money Laundering Regulations 1993 which makes disclosure about suspicions of money laundering compulsory. Other persons who receive knowledge of money laundering in the course of business are required to disclose or face prosecution for an offence under ss49, 50, 51 and 52 of the Drug Trafficking Act 1994, ss93A, 93B or 93C of the Criminal Justice Act 1988 (as amended), or ss11 or 18 of the Prevention of Terrorism (Temporary Provisions) Act 1989. In common with most European countries the UK has suspicion-based legislation as oppose to the American system which has a monetary level currently $10,000 above which transactions must be reported – there does not appear to be any evidence that either is more successful than the other.

The Regulations will not catch all of the people engaged in money laundering, the big launderers will find ways of circumventing any regulations to cover their activity, ensuring it is simply not disclosed, but as a result of the various disclosure legislation over 15,000 reports were received by NCIS in 1994.

Tipping Off in Respect of Disclosures

Tipping off is an offence which is split into three parts, first where a disclosure has been made to a constable, secondly where a disclosure has been made to any person and thirdly where a constable is investigating a money laundering offence. In this section we will deal with the disclosure offences only. 'Tipping off' is an offence reflected in all three Acts and basically is telling any person any information which prejudices the disclosure, or any investigation or proposed investigation into such disclosure.

Section 53 Drug Trafficking Act 1994

Points to Prove
- s53(1) The person charged knew that a constable is acting or proposing to act in a drug money laundering investigation which is being or is about to be conducted; or

- s53(2) The person charged knows a disclosure has been made to a constable; or
- s53(3) The person charged knows or suspects such a disclosure has been made to any person; and
- That the person charged discloses to any person information or any other matter which is likely to prejudice the investigation, proposed investigation, the disclosure, or any investigation conducted following the disclosure.

Maximum Penalty
On conviction on indictment, 5 years' imprisonment, a fine or both; summarily, 6 months' imprisonment, a fine to the statutory maximum or both.

Section 93D Criminal Justice Act 1988 (as amended)
Points to Prove
- s93D(1) The person charged knew that a constable is acting or proposing to act in a money laundering investigation which is being or is about to be conducted; or
- s93D(2) The person charged knows a disclosure has been made to a constable or knows or suspects a constable is proposing to investigate a disclosure; or
- s93D(3) The person charged knows a disclosure has been made to any person; and
- He discloses to any person information or any other matter which is likely to prejudice the investigation, proposed investigation, the disclosure or prejudice any investigation which may follow the disclosure.

Maximum Penalty
On conviction on indictment, 5 years' imprisonment, a fine or both; summarily, 6 months' imprisonment, a fine to the statutory maximum or both.

Chapter 2 – Regulations, Disclosures & Tipping Off

Section 17 Prevention of Terrorism (Temporary Provisions) Act 1989

Points to Prove

- A person knows or has reasonable cause to suspect that an investigation is taking place or a disclosure has been made; and
- Makes any disclosure which is likely to prejudice the investigation; or
- Falsifies, conceals, or destroys, or disposes of, or permits any of the same acts to material which is relevant to the investigation.

Maximum Penalty

On conviction on indictment, 5 years' imprisonment, a fine or both; summarily, 6 months' imprisonment, a fine to statutory maximum or both.

In examining the offence of 'tipping off' it should be born in mind that as a disclosure can only come about in the course of business then the offence of 'tipping off' must relate to a business-type disclosure. An example could be:

Mandy is told by her friend Barney that he intends to disclose to police that his friend Joanna is laundering her drug trafficking money through an account at a local bank. None of the parties involved have come by the information in the course of business. Mandy now intends to tell or 'tip off' Joanna about Barney making the disclosure. The disclosure to police by Barney would be information about a crime not a disclosure for the purposes of any of the Acts. Mandy would not commit the offence of 'tipping off' in respect of a disclosure but would commit a 'tipping off' offence in respect of an investigation or proposed investigation into drug trafficking money laundering (s53(1)(a) of the Drug Trafficking Act 1994). If, however, Barney had come across the information about Joanna in the course of employment or business then the tipping off would have been in respect of a disclosure and therefore an offence against s53(2) of the Drug Trafficking Act 1994 is committed because the disclosure was to the police.

There is a further anomaly within the disclosure legislation where the legal privilege aspect rears its head again, that is in relation to 'tipping off'. In the Acts there is a clause which states:

Nothing makes it an offence for a professional legal adviser to disclose any information or other matter to a client in connection with the giving of legal advice, or to any person in contemplation of, or in connection with legal proceedings and for the purpose of those proceedings. This privilege is again negated if there is a view to a criminal purpose.

An example of a legal privilege 'tipping off' could be:

During an investigation into a money laundering offence a police officer serves an order on a bank who hold a mortgage account, obtained dubiously as an attempt at layering the proceeds of drugs. The bank now wish to foreclose on that loan and take a civil action to recover their money. The bank starts a civil action that would entail tipping off the client in the contents of this action, they would under this clause be within the law to do so. *(For further information on Legal Privilege see page 52.)*

In conclusion then in order to protect disclosure information being prejudiced at any time by any person the offence of 'tipping off' is created. This offence imposes on any person the need to keep information about a disclosure secret to the point that no client or party to the disclosure is informed of it, an institution could not confirm that such a disclosure existed, even if the client posed the question. The practice within most organisations would be to respond to any such inquiry with the reply that because of the legislation the institution concerned is unable to confirm or deny that such a disclosure exists. This would be the case even if the client knew from some other party that the institution had disclosed the information.

The disclosure of information is an important weapon in the fight against the unlawful laundering of the proceeds of drugs, crime and terrorism. Disclosures must be made and investigated in confidence both inside and outside the organisations concerned. Breach of such confidence renders the persons responsible to a sentence of imprisonment, it is both criminally and morally unacceptable.

Chapter 3
Searches & Social Profiling

Chapter 3
Searches & Social Profiling

Whether investigating a money launderer or the conduct of a criminal their finances generally hold the key to a successful discovery of hidden assets. Whatever the crime a financial examination into the individual's monetary affairs will usually prove invaluable. Apart from the finances of actual suspects of crime being of great utility, a similar profile could assist in other inquiries. For example, many a murder victim has been the subject of blackmail or other nefarious activity, sometimes unknown to relatives and friends. A social profile using the individual's financial affairs as a base can be of tremendous importance and ultimately an efficient weapon in detecting motives of crime.

'You see the stone hit the water because it splashes. As it begins to sink, the water ripples and, for a few moments, you can still find the spot where the stone hit. But as the stone sinks deeper, the ripples fade. By the time the stone reaches the bottom, any traces of it are long gone and the stone itself may be impossible to find. That's exactly what happens to laundered money,' (*The Laundrymen* by Jeffrey Robinson).

This vivid analogy beautifully describes the result of an efficient money laundering enterprise. It is the task of the financial investigator to discover the audit trail and ultimately the tainted proceeds of crime in whatever form it has been integrated. Discovering these assets is a difficult job especially when the launderer is using sophisticated methods to layer the money. Launderers are aware of the difficulties the investigator will encounter when trying to elicit information from abroad *(see pages 141-143)*.

The source of 'searches' open to a financial investigator are extremely important. It is equally important that these sources be protected, it would therefore be remiss, disloyal and naive of us to publish these in a book. Money launderers and criminals are resourceful individuals and would benefit greatly if such sources were made public.

It is important to realise that the task of the financial investigator can be eased and the final result of such an inquiry improved by the actions of personnel coming into original contact with the suspect or victim. They should look for and take details of bank and building society accounts, telephone numbers, alias', addresses used, vehicles owned or seen in, associate names and addresses, membership cards, company name(s) and other financial or asset-related documentation; and pass it on to the financial investigator or intelligence gatherer. Even the smallest piece of information can turn a mundane inquiry into a major money-laundering investigation. The missing piece of the jig-saw maybe that telephone number written on the wall next to the telephone or the number on a scrap of paper may hide a bank account. This information-gathering exercise may have to be done surreptitiously in order to preserve an audit trail or the element of surprise.

More often than not the financial investigator will be asked to carry out their research some time after the original matter came to notice. It maybe that a disclosure under the Money Laundering Regulations 1993 needs working on, or an informant may have given information about an individual apparently involved in crime, or it maybe that a 'prosecutor's statement' *(see Chapter 7)* has to be prepared on a person arrested for drug trafficking or crime.

Whether conducting a proactive or reactive financial investigation, it is essential that the investigator carries out searches of various indices and other relevant sources. At the outset the investigator must not ignore the Attorney General's guidelines concerning 'unused material' and the Criminal Procedure and Investigations Act 1996. Under this legislation the prosecution has a duty to disclose material, at the primary stage, which in the prosecutor's opinion undermines the prosecution case. At the secondary stage, which is after the accused has served a defence statement, the prosecutor must disclose any material which might reasonably be expected to assist the accused's case.

'Unused material' is defined as all material coming into possession or control of the prosecution, therefore the financial investigator's inquiry notes may, despite arguing that such material was not created for evidential purposes, be disclosable at both the primary or secondary stages. It is suggested that all

Chapter 3 – Searches & Social Profiling

material obtained and created by the financial investigation officer is disclosable to the defence. The financial investigator should send a schedule of their material to the Disclosure Officer who can attach them to forms MG6C and MG6D as appropriate, and forward them to the reviewing lawyer. (Forms MG6C and MG6D are part of the nationally approved Crown Prosecution case papers.)

In the case of sensitive material the prosecution will apply to the court for an order that the material should not be disclosed to the defence on the grounds of public interest immunity. Confidential information such as disclosures under the Money Laundering Regulations 1993 come within the definition of sensitive material. It is important to realise that the courts will have to settle arguments around this new legislation. Exact procedures to be adopted in relation to unused material will be known to all financial investigators. If there is any doubt advice should be sought from the Crown Prosecution Service responsible for the accused's prosecution.

This maybe particularly pertinent if a proactive intelligence-gathering investigation turns into a prosecution. It is imperative, therefore, that an accurate and systematic record of all searches is kept.

A simple search checklist, search schedule and neat filing system instigated at the outset of an inquiry will prevent the accidental loss of information and enable the investigator to produce accurate work. The financial investigator may be carrying out several different inquires at once and therefore it is imperative to approach such an inquiry systematically.

Some financial investigators have a pre-prepared financial profile or lifestyle booklet which can be used as both an aide-memoir when questioning suspects or a record for searches. With experience it will be easy enough to compile such a booklet. The booklet will contain the personal and financial details of the suspect together with a completed checklist of all inquires undertaken by the financial investigator, including those inquiries which necessitated a production order or warrant *(see Chapter 4)*. At the conclusion the financial investigator should compile an objective summary of the profile.

It is unnecessary for the financial investigator to make a check of every conceivable source on every financial investigation, there is a need to prioritise searches. This can only be achieved by adopting a pragmatic approach and by using empirical knowledge gained through experience. It is most important that experienced financial investigators pass on their expertise and are always available to brief and train colleagues who may be faced with the gathering of money laundering and confiscation material. For example, an opportunity for a financial investigator to be part of a pre-operation briefing could ultimately reap rich rewards and save time tracing assets and possible evidence.

There are countless methods of laundering money, every fresh piece of legislation designed to thwart the launderer stimulates new and resourceful ways of circumventing the legislation. Whatever method is used to launder money the financial investigator has to be equally resourceful in discovering the audit trail and consequent source of illicit finances. The financial investigator has to be sceptical about every piece of information they discover, and by applying an inquiring mind to the information the launderers activities will be discovered. The financial investigator needs to be aware of common methods of laundering and then realise that these can be adapted to any circumstance or jurisdiction.

For instance, a large number of individuals, known as 'Smurfs', can open bank accounts and feed in lots of small amounts of cash. In due course all the accounts can be drawn upon raising no suspicion. Another method is the setting up of companies and then raising invoices between those companies for fictitious business transactions, thereby introducing illicit money to pay for them.

Business fronts that deal in a service or raw cash are ideal for inflating and/or inventing proceeds. The financial investigator should constantly query suspect business accounts and never accept invoices at face value.

Underground Banking

It is important that the financial investigator is aware of the existence of global 'underground banking' systems. Underground banking pre-dates the established formal system that we are all aware of. Underground banking tends to be culturally based and probably originated in the Asian subcontinent. Hawalla, Hindi or Chitti Banking are three of the

Chapter 3 – Searches & Social Profiling

most common names for underground banking. The system depends heavily on trust which if abused usually results in serious consequences.

Underground banks do not currently commit offences against UK banking or financial legislation, however they do fail to abide by the Money Laundering Regulations 1993 and other disclosure legislation (*see Chapters 2 and 5*). Wherever they operate, underground banks avoid tax and exchange control regulations, when in force. Because of their secrecy, underground banks are tailor-made for criminals to finance their activities or launder their dishonest proceeds. Underground banks are used for legitimate reasons to transfer credit from one country to another, however if they are over-used the country's economy can be seriously effected. The country will be starved of much- needed tax revenue and foreign currency as well as the employment in formal banking being threatened.

Let us look at a simple example of how the concept of underground banking works:

1. I am going to India for my holidays and instead of going to the bank for travellers cheques, paying commission, I go to my underground bank and hand over my sterling spending money.

2. In exchange I am given half a playing card (a cloakroom ticket or something similar). The other half of the playing card, which is torn in front of me, is retained by the banker and I give the banker details of when and where I require rupees.

3. I travel to India with my half of playing card.

4. I am contacted and visited by someone with the other half of playing card. The two halves are put together and if they fit I receive my rupees, minus a much smaller amount of commission than the formal rate and/or a much better exchange rate. (I have used India as an example but it could be any other country of the world.)

5. In India there will be nationals wanting to travel to the UK, they will attend their underground bank in India and give rupees. Exactly the same process as above will occur however the Indian will be given sterling when visited by the banker's assistant in the UK.

Note: No money leaves the originating country.

There are many different variations of underground banking some known and others unknown. It is sufficient for the financial investigator to be aware of the concept of secret banking because the audit trail of some inquiries has in the past dried up for no apparent reason. Perhaps the suspect has used the services of an underground bank?

Chapter 4
Production Orders & Warrants

Chapter 4
Production Orders & Warrants

After an introduction and commentary on the relevant legislation there are a number of schematic flowcharts to assist in understanding the important sections.

Production orders are a judge's direction to produce or give access to material held under a civil duty of confidentiality. They are obtainable under the following legislation:

- Section 93H of the Criminal Justice Act 1988 as amended by Proceeds of Crime Act 1995.
- Section 55 of the Drug Trafficking Act 1994.
- Section 17 and schedule 7 of the Prevention of Terrorism Act 1989.
- Section 9 and schedule 1 of the Police and Criminal Evidence Act 1984.

Material stored on computer is in addition obtainable by virtue of s28(3) of the Data Protection Act 1984, using a written request. Unlike the above legislation under which production orders can be obtained, this Act gives little protection to persons who reply, and allows action against them for breaching a confidentiality. It is not surprising therefore that data requests are not legally enforceable.

In addition to the above powers available to a 'constable' to seek production orders and warrants, the High Court may 'on an application by the person appearing to the court to have conduct of any prosecution', order the disclosure of information held by a Government Department. This must be for the purposes of facilitating restraint, charging orders or the realisation of property. Those powers can be found under the following legislation:

- Section 93J of the Criminal Justice Act 1988 as amended by Proceeds of Crime Act 1995.
- Section 59 of the Drug Trafficking Act 1994.

Production orders allow the holder of confidential information to disclose it without risk of breaching the duty of confidentiality. If satisfied that the access conditions apply a Circuit Judge may order the holder of the material to produce it or give access to it. Compliance is required with such an order despite any other civil or criminal statute under which they may hold the material. The types of material to which orders may apply vary but could include customer documents held by banks and other financial institutions. The material may not directly relate to the crime but could be of substantial value to the investigation. A production order may be used as a proactive weapon for investigating crime and criminals or a reactive tool for discovering the assets of criminals. Used as a reactive tool production orders can facilitate the financial investigator to compile the prosecutor's statement in order that the judge can make an accurate confiscation order.

The confidentiality appertaining to the material always remains with the party who originally gave over the material in confidence. The original party may decide to relinquish the confidentiality, if this occurs it is advisable to obtain such a change in written form. This course must be explored in all cases in order to comply with paragraph 2(b), schedule 1, of the Police and Criminal Evidence Act 1984, 'that all other methods have been tried without success or were not tried because they were bound to fail'.

Under the same paragraph of the Police and Criminal Evidence Act 1984 police are bound to apply for an order under the Criminal Justice Act 1988. If an application fails under the Criminal Justice Act 1988 it may be possible that an application under schedule 1 of the Police and Criminal Evidence Act 1984 maybe successful. The stricter access conditions under PACE would however need to be met.

When faced with cases concerning confidential material consider the case of *Marcel & others v Metropolitan Police Commissioner* (1991). Here the court decided police had a duty of care and confidentiality over items seized under a PACE warrant or order that was identical to that of the owner. This resulted because under PACE the owner remained entitled to a copy of the documents and therefore retained their ownership even when police had possession of the material. The police and all persons have a duty to comply with any court order or the directions of a judge. The owner of the material is allowed to make representations at any hearing. Police have a

Chapter 4 – Production Orders & Warrants

duty to give interested parties to the material a notice of any court proceedings. The police should therefore never disclose documents obtained by virtue of production orders or warrants unless:

- Ordered to do so by a judge; or
- Consent of the owner has been obtained to take such action; or
- Disclosure is necessary in order to carry out police duties in relation to an investigation or prosecution.

Production orders and warrants are unobtainable in respect of material subject to legal privilege. 'Legal professional privilege is paramount', *R v Derby Magistrates' Court* (1995). However, see s10 of the Police and Criminal Evidence Act 1984 below. Similarly, in all applications except terrorism, neither can excluded material be obtained. See ss11 to 13 of the Police and Criminal Evidence Act 1984 below.

The Police and Criminal Evidence Act 1984 defines confidential material as 'Special Procedure Material'. See s14 of the Police and Criminal Evidence Act 1984 below.

Definitions – Special Procedure Material

Section 14 Police and Criminal Evidence Act 1984
Defines special procedure material as material held on a confidential basis but not excluded material or material subject to legal privilege including journalistic material which is not excluded material.

Section 14(2) Police and Criminal Evidence Act 1984
This further defines special procedure material as material subject to an express or implied undertaking of confidentiality or a statutory restriction on disclosure or obligation of secrecy, by someone who acquired or created it in the course of a trade, business, profession, or occupation or for the purpose of any office whether paid or unpaid.

Examples
Statutory restriction on disclosure
Would apply to documents subject to a legal requirement to remain confidential such as those held under the Official Secrets Act.

Obligation of secrecy
Would apply to material held by a bank, solicitor or accountant on behalf of a client with merely an implied confidential relationship.

Section 14(3), (4), and (5) Police and Criminal Evidence Act 1984
Provides that material that was special procedure material remains so even when passed between employees or companies who may not be aware of the confidentiality. An example might be a client's material passed between accountants within an accountancy firm.

Special procedure material cannot be created by an employer telling employees that any company records are confidential. Material is only special procedure material if it was such immediately prior to the acquisition of such material.

Definitions – Legal Privilege

Section 10(1) Police and Criminal Evidence Act 1984
Defines items subject to legal privilege as:
i) communications between a professional legal adviser and his client, or any person representing his client, in connection with the giving of legal advice
ii) communications between the same, [as i) above], and any other person, in connection with or in contemplation of legal proceedings, for the purpose of such proceedings
iii) items enclosed with, or referred to in, communications in connection with i) and ii) above, when they are in possession of persons entitled to possession of them.

Examples
Communication between a legal adviser in connection with the giving of legal advice
This need not be connected with pending proceedings and would include documents sent between parties purely for advice such as a draft contract.

Chapter 4 – Production Orders & Warrants

Communication between lawyer and client when proceedings are pending
This is much wider as it includes any other person and would include communications with third parties. The sending of documents to a professional witness such as an accountant for advice would be an example and the documents would be items enclosed in connection with legal proceedings.

Section 10(2) Police and Criminal Evidence Act 1984
States that 'items held by any person with the intention of furthering a criminal purpose are not "items" subject to legal privilege' but become purely special procedure material. They are therefore accessible by production orders or warrants. Items that would be the subject of legal privilege but by virtue of s10(2) of the Police and Criminal Evidence Act 1984 are items held in furtherance of a criminal purpose, revert to special procedure material, and therefore require a judge's order or warrant. (See *R v Guildhall Justices ex parte Primlaks Holdings* (1989) where a Serious Fraud Office application found such special procedure material under a s8 PACE search warrant granted by a JP from a magistrates' court.) Where such items are sought which require a judge's order or warrant alongside others for which a magistrate could issue a warrant then a judge should deal with the application in its entirety.

In the case *R v Central Criminal Court, ex parte Francis & Francis (a law firm)* (1988) a central drug squad officer applied for an order under the now repealed s27 of the Drug Trafficking Offences Act 1986 requiring solicitors Francis & Francis to provide all files relating to a client Mrs G. The allegation concerned a drug trafficker who laundered the proceeds through Mrs G. a member of the family and her flower shop business purchased for £330,000. The court accepted Mrs G. was an innocent party. Her solicitors who carried out the conveyancing were also an innocent party. This case made several important rulings:

- The critical point in time arises when the communication is made, did someone have a criminal purpose in mind? If so, legal privilege is negated.

- Criminal purpose does not have to be specific it is enough to have the intent to 'salt away' the proceeds of a serious crime or money laundering.

- The principle of legal privilege should not be used to protect the perpetrators of serious crimes.
- The legal privilege would only be lost if the parties were using the solicitors or clients as a duped innocent tool or the legal adviser was criminally involved.

In the case of *R v Inner London Sessions Crown Court, ex parte Baines & Baines (Solicitors)* (1988) police were seeking information on the purchase of properties surrounding the Brinks-Mat Ltd robbery at Heathrow Airport. The court held that the records of a conveyancing transaction were not privileged since they were not in connection with advice and were for the purpose of a public record, although correspondence contained in the file might be subject to privilege. The Law Society recommends that solicitor's receiving production orders examine files and prepare lists of documents on which privilege is claimed and serves same on police and judge in order to oppose any order for production.

In the previously mentioned *Primlaks Holdings* case it was held that documents pre-existing the legal privilege could not attain privilege by sending them to solicitors.

Remember: legal privilege is that of the client and can be revoked by the client.

Definitions – Excluded Material

Section 11(1) Police and Criminal Evidence Act 1984
Defines excluded material as three types: personal records, samples of human tissue or tissue fluid, and journalistic material. These are further defined in the sections mentioned below.

Personal Records – s12(a)
Are records acquired in course of trade, business, profession or other occupation and held in confidence. They must be documents or records making it possible to identify individuals and which relate to physical or mental health or spiritual counselling for personal welfare.

In *R v Cardiff Crown Court, ex parte Kellam* (1993) hospital records were held to be excluded material.

This section plainly covers the caring professions such as doctor's records, citizens' advice, probation, social workers and the clergy. However, the section is far wider and includes school records and lesser known cult's records such as Hare Krishna that may relate to counselling or personal welfare.

Human Tissue or Tissue Fluid – s12(b)

Taken for the purpose of prognosis or medical treatment. Human tissue and tissue fluid do not present problems of interpretation, it includes the contents from a stomach, and any samples given for examination, but may not cover the bullet from a wound, even if contaminated by fluids or tissue.

When examining the rights of an individual over material one should ascertain the ownership of the confidentiality. In *R v Singleton* (1995) a dentist volunteered dental mouth impressions of a patient who was convicted on the evidence in the records. The Court of Appeal held it was the confidence of the maker of the record or record holder that needed safeguarding, not the suspect, therefore the dentist was at liberty to give up the records without an order.

Journalistic Material – s13

Anything that comes into being or is acquired for purpose of journalism (paid or unpaid or however humble) and is held in confidence.

Journalistic material in most cases is for publication and therefore not held in confidence. However, when an express condition of confidentiality is placed on the details by the author, then this part only would be excluded journalistic material. Journalistic material that is not excluded will be special procedure material by virtue of s14(1)(b) PACE.

The Crown Prosecution Service must be consulted in any case where there is likely to be an issue over items subject to legal privilege or excluded material.

Production orders are orders of a Crown Court Judge, therefore failure to comply with an order is contempt of the Crown Court. Such a contempt may form the basis for a production warrant *(see Production Warrants)*. The person responsible for the contempt may be ordered to the court to answer their contempt.

In order to ascertain the correct production order the following schematic flowcharts may assist. However, the following cases, *R v Guildford Crown Court, ex parte Director of Public Prosecutions* (1996) and *R v Southwark Crown Court, ex parte Bowles* (1996), are currently causing much debate and must be researched fully as at the time of publishing this book, they await judicial review.

Chapter 4 – Production Orders & Warrants

Production Orders as of 1.11.95

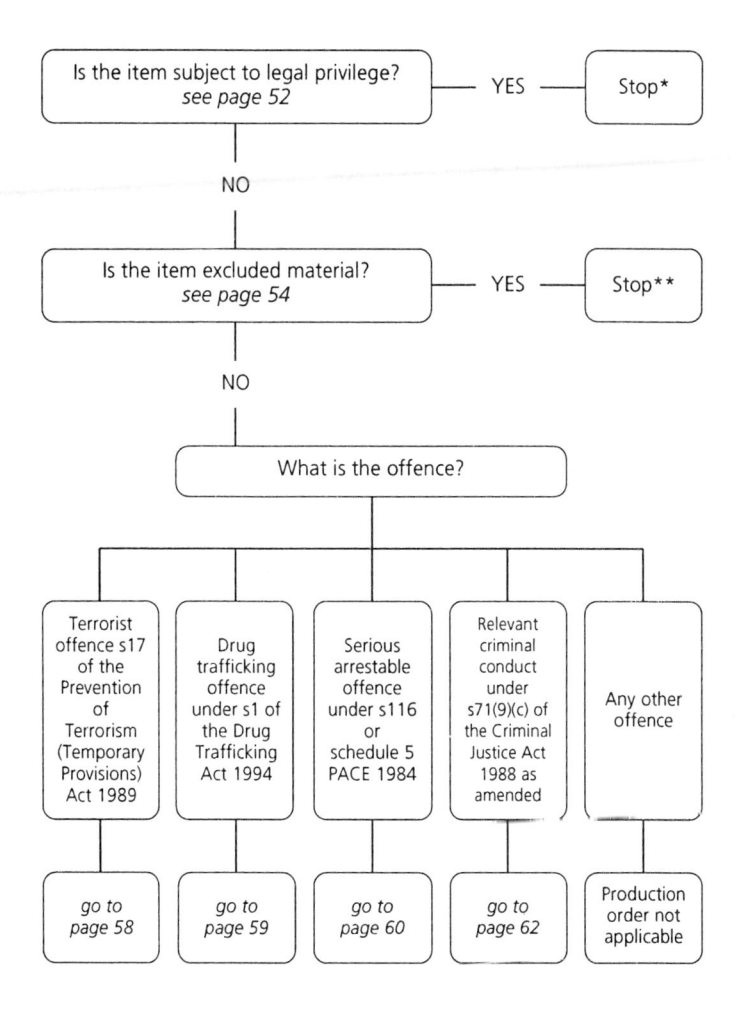

```
Is the item subject to legal privilege?  — YES — Stop*
see page 52
         │
         NO
         │
Is the item excluded material?  — YES — Stop**
see page 54
         │
         NO
         │
What is the offence?
```

- Terrorist offence s17 of the Prevention of Terrorism (Temporary Provisions) Act 1989 → *go to page 58*
- Drug trafficking offence under s1 of the Drug Trafficking Act 1994 → *go to page 59*
- Serious arrestable offence under s116 or schedule 5 PACE 1984 → *go to page 60*
- Relevant criminal conduct under s71(9)(c) of the Criminal Justice Act 1988 as amended → *go to page 62*
- Any other offence → Production order not applicable

---

* *Cannot be searched for or seized under any legislation.*
** *Cannot be obtained unless prior to PACE 1984 a warrant could be obtained (eg stolen property) or the case is a terrorist offence.*

Schedule 7 Prevention of Terrorism (Temporary Provisions) Act 1989

A constable may apply to a Circuit Judge for an order providing:

- It is a terrorist investigation defined under s17 of the Prevention of Terrorism Act 1989. Investigations into:
  - Commission, preparation or instigation of offences under s14 which includes:
    Membership of a proscribed organisation (s2). Failing to abide by exclusion order (s8). Contributions towards acts of terrorism (s9). Contributions towards proscribed organisations (s10). Assisting in the retention or control of terrorist funds (s11).
  - Any act in furtherance of or in connection with:
    Membership of a proscribed organisation (s2). Contributions towards acts of terrorism (s9). Contributions towards proscribed organisations (s10). Assisting in the retention or control of terrorist funds (s11). Failing to give information concerning terrorist acts (s18).
  - The resources of a proscribed organisation.
  - Investigations into proscribing an organisation by application to the Home Secretary.

- The material is in existence or it will be within 28 days of the date of the order.

- The material to which the application relates consists of special procedure or excluded material and does not include material subject to legal privilege.

- The material whether on its own or together with other material is likely to be of substantial value to the investigation.

- There are reasonable grounds for believing that it is in the public interest, having regard to:
  - the benefit likely to accrue the investigation if the material is produced
  - the circumstances under which the person in possession holds the material that the material should be produced or access given to it.

- If on such application the judge is satisfied he may make an order that the person who appears to possess the

Chapter 4 – Production Orders & Warrants

material shall produce it to a constable within 7 days or other such longer or shorter period as appropriate, and if that material is not in the person's possession then to state to the best of their knowledge or belief where it is.

- The judge on application may grant access to premises to obtain access to material.
- Where material is contained in computer the material must be produced in a readable form which can be taken away.
- Application may be made ex parte to a judge in Chambers.
- An order shall have effect notwithstanding any other obligation as to secrecy imposed by statute or otherwise.
- May be made in relation to material possessed by a Government Department that is an authorised department for purposes of the Crown Proceedings Act 1947.

Section 55 Drug Trafficking Act 1994 Production Order

A constable may apply to a Circuit Judge for an order providing:

- There are reasonable grounds for suspecting a specified person has carried on or benefited from drug trafficking (defined in s1 of the Drug Trafficking Act 1994).
- There are reasonable grounds for suspecting that the material to which the application relates:
  - is likely to be of substantial value (whether by itself or together with other material) to the investigation for purposes of which application is made; and
  - does not consist of or include items subject to legal privilege or excluded material.
- There are reasonable grounds for believing that it is in the public interest, having regard:
  - to the benefit likely to accrue to the investigation if the material is obtained; and
  - to the circumstances under which the person in possession of the material holds it.

  That material should be produced or access given to it.

- If, on such an application, the judge is satisfied that the

conditions are fulfiled, he may make an order that the person who appears to him to be in possession of the material to which the application relates shall:
- produce it to a constable for him to take away, or
- give a constable access to it, within 7 days unless it appears to the judge that a longer or shorter period is appropriate.

I Judge on application by constable may grant entry to premises to obtain access to material.

I Where material is contained in computer the material must be produced in a form which is readable and can be taken away.

I Application may be made ex parte to a judge in Chambers.

I Shall have effect notwithstanding any obligation as to secrecy or other restriction upon the disclosure of information imposed by statute or otherwise; and

I May be made in relation to material possessed by an authorised government department that is an authorised department for the purposes of the Crown Proceedings Act 1947.

I References to 'a person benefiting from any criminal conduct', in relation to conduct which is not an offence because it is outside the jurisdiction, shall apply as if it had occurred in England and Wales, and shall be construed as if it had so occurred in the UK. *See Appendix I for sample format of application.*

Schedule 9 PACE
Serious Arrestable Offence Production Order

A constable may apply to a Circuit Judge for an order providing:

I There are reasonable grounds for believing, a serious arrestable offence as in schedule 5 or section 116 has been committed, and there is special procedure material, or includes excluded material that could have been obtained prior to PACE by virtue of a search warrant, on the premises specified on the application.

Chapter 4 – Production Orders & Warrants

- That the material to which the application relates:
  - is likely to be of substantial value (whether by itself or with other material) to the investigation, and
  - that the material is likely to be relevant evidence.
- Other methods of obtaining the material:
  - have been tried without success; or
  - has not been tried because it appeared they were bound to fail; and
- There are reasonable grounds for believing that it is in the public interest, having regard to the benefit likely to accrue to the investigation if the material is obtained, and to the circumstances under which the person in possession of the material holds it.
  That material should be produced or access given to it.
- If, on such an application, the judge is satisfied that the conditions are fulfiled, he may make an order that the person who appears to him to be in possession of the material to which the application relates shall:
  - produce it to a constable for him to take away, or
  - give a constable access to it, within 7 days unless it appears to the judge that a longer or shorter period is appropriate.
- Material produced shall be treated as if it were material seized by a constable.
- Where material is contained in a computer the material must be produced in a form which is readable and can be taken away.

All applications must be inter parte and notice of such served on all interested parties to the application.

Any person receiving an order or notice of such shall not conceal, destroy, alter or dispose of material without leave of the judge or written permission of a constable.

PACE orders require the authority of a Superintendent or suitably authorised Chief Inspector.

Failure to comply with an order is contempt of the Crown Court but see Production Warrants *(page 63)*.

Section 93H Criminal Justice Act 1988 Production Orders

A constable may, apply to a Circuit Judge for an order providing:

- It is an offence to which section 71(9)(c) of this Act applies from which any person has benefited.

- A constable is conducting an investigation into whether any person has benefited or the extent or whereabouts of such benefit is sought.

- There are reasonable grounds for suspecting that the material to which the application relates:
  - is likely to be of substantial value (whether by itself or together with other material) to the investigation for the purposes of which application is made; and
  - does not consist of or include items subject to legal privilege or excluded material.

- There are reasonable grounds for believing that it is in the public interest, having regard:
  - to the benefit likely to accrue to the investigation if the material is obtained, and
  - to the circumstances under which person in possession of the material holds it, that the material should be produced or access given to it.

- Judge, on the application of a constable, may grant entry to the premises to obtain access to the material.

- Where material is contained in a computer the material must be produced in a readable form that can be taken away.

- Application may be made ex parte to a judge in Chambers.

- An order shall have effect notwithstanding any obligation as to secrecy or other restriction upon the disclosure of information imposed by statute or otherwise.

- May be made in relation to material in the possession of an authorised government department that is an authorised department for the purposes of the Crown Proceedings Act 1947.

Chapter 4 – Production Orders & Warrants

- References to a person benefiting from any criminal conduct, in relation to conduct which is not an offence because it occurred outside the jurisdiction, shall be construed as if it had so occurred in the UK. *See Appendix I for suggested format of application.*

Production Warrants

Production warrants are obtainable under the following Acts and sections:

- Section 93I of the Criminal Justice Act 1988 as amended by Proceeds of Crime Act 1995.
- Section 56 of the Drug Trafficking Act 1994.
- Section 17 and schedule 7 of the Prevention of Terrorism Act 1989.
- Section 9 and schedule 1 of the Police and Criminal Evidence Act 1984.

In order to obtain a production warrant the conditions relating to production orders must first be satisfied. Then certain further conditions are applicable and a judge must be satisfied that these are all complied with before issuing a warrant. The following flowcharts *(see overleaf)* describe the areas that must be complied with in order to obtain a production warrant.

When considering using a production warrant remember that there is no onus on the person to produce the material it is up to the officer executing same to look for the material. This in itself may present problems particularly if the premises are over a number of floors and the material is similarly spread. The warrants under drug and crime legislation may include named persons to accompany officers, this is particularly useful where the material sought is of a nature that has to be valued or identified such as antiques or paintings. This course is also useful where the premises themselves need to be valued, to ascertain the benefit applicable to property owned by the person charged, in these circumstances an estate agent or valuer may be the named person who accompanies the officer.

Schedule 7 Prevention of Terrorism (Temporary Provisions) Act 1989
Section 5(1) Production Warrant

A constable may apply to a Circuit Judge for a warrant providing:

- A production order under s4(3) has not been complied with.

- There are reasonable grounds for believing that there is on the premises material consisting of or including excluded material or special procedure material which does not include items subject of legal privilege.

- A terrorist investigation is being carried out.

- The material is of substantial benefit to the investigation.

- It is in the public interest having regard to the circumstances in which it is held and the benefit likely to accrue to the investigation if the material is obtained. It should be produced or access given to it.

- It would not be appropriate to issue a production order in respect of the material because:
    - it is not practicable to communicate with any person entitled to produce the material; or
    - it is not practicable to communicate with any person entitled to grant access to the material or entitled to grant entry to the premises; or
    - the investigation would be seriously prejudiced unless a constable could secure immediate access to the material.

- A warrant under this section shall authorise a constable to enter premises and search the premises specified or any person therein and to seize and retain anything found thereon or on any person, other than items subject to legal privilege, which may be of substantial value (either by itself or together with other material) to the investigation for the purposes of which the application was made.

Chapter 4 -- Production Orders & Warrants

Section 56 Drug Trafficking Act 1994 Warrant to Search

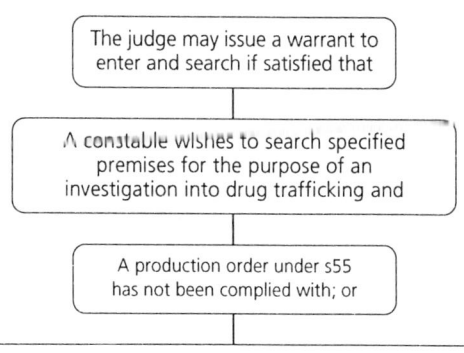

The judge may issue a warrant to enter and search if satisfied that

A constable wishes to search specified premises for the purpose of an investigation into drug trafficking and

A production order under s55 has not been complied with; or

That there are reasonable grounds to suspect that a specified person has carried on or benefited from drug trafficking; and

There are reasonable grounds for suspecting the material to which the application relates:
i) is likely to be of substantial value (whether by itself or with other material) to the investigation, and
ii) does not consist of or include items subject to legal privilege or excluded material; and

There are reasonable grounds for believing that it is in the public interest, having regard:
i) to the benefit likely to accrue to the investigation if the material is obtained, and
ii) to the circumstances under which the person in possession of the material holds it.

That material should be produced or access given, but it is not practicable to make a production order because:
i) it is not practicable to communicate with any person entitled to produce the material; or
ii) it is not practicable to communicate with any person entitled to grant access to the material or premises on which the material is situated; or
iii) the investigation for the purposes of which the application is made might be seriously prejudiced unless a constable arriving at the premises could secure immediate access to the material; or

continued on next page

continued from previous page

That there are reasonable grounds for suspecting that a specified person has benefited from drug trafficking; and
i) There are reasonable grounds for suspecting that there is on the premises any such material relating;
ii) to the specified person; or
iii) to drug trafficking that is likely to be of substantial value (whether by itself or together with other material) to the investigation for the purpose of which the application is made but the material cannot at the time of the application be particularised; and that:

i) it is not practicable to communicate with any person entitled to grant entry to the premises, or
ii) entry to the premises will not be granted unless a warrant is produced; or
iii) the investigation for the purposes of which the application is made might be seriously prejudiced unless a constable arriving at the premises could secure immediate entry to them; and

Where a constable has entered premises in the execution of a warrant, he may seize and retain any material, other than items subject to legal privilege or excluded material, which is likely to be of substantial value (whether by itself or together with other material) to the investigation for the purpose of which the warrant was issued.

See Appendix I for suggested format of application.

Chapter 4 – Production Orders & Warrants

Schedule 1 PACE
Production Warrants

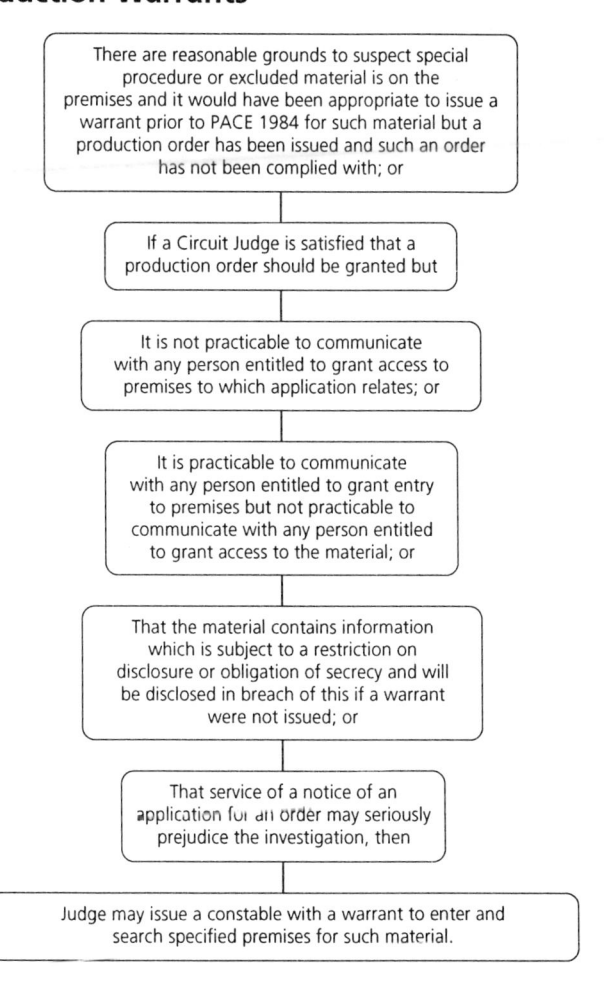

> There are reasonable grounds to suspect special procedure or excluded material is on the premises and it would have been appropriate to issue a warrant prior to PACE 1984 for such material but a production order has been issued and such an order has not been complied with; or

> If a Circuit Judge is satisfied that a production order should be granted but

> It is not practicable to communicate with any person entitled to grant access to premises to which application relates; or

> It is practicable to communicate with any person entitled to grant entry to premises but not practicable to communicate with any person entitled to grant access to the material; or

> That the material contains information which is subject to a restriction on disclosure or obligation of secrecy and will be disclosed in breach of this if a warrant were not issued; or

> That service of a notice of an application for an order may seriously prejudice the investigation, then

> Judge may issue a constable with a warrant to enter and search specified premises for such material.

Under PACE Codes of Practice Code B para 5:13, warrants issued under this schedule must be executed by a person of the rank of Inspector or above.

Section 93I Criminal Justice Act 1988 Production Warrant

> A judge may issue a warrant authorising a constable to enter and search premises if satisfied that

> A constable is conducting an investigation into whether any person has benefited from any criminal conduct or into the extent or whereabouts of the proceeds of any criminal conduct, in relation to specified premises; and

> That a section 93H production order has not been complied with; or

a) That there are reasonable grounds for suspecting that a specified person has benefited from criminal conduct; and

b) There are reasonable grounds for suspecting that the material to which the application relates:
   - is likely to be of substantial value (whether by itself or together with other material) to the investigation for the purposes of which the application is made; and
   - does not consist of or include items subject to legal privilege or excluded material; and

There are reasonable grounds for believing that it is in the public interest, having regard:

a) to the benefit likely to accrue to the investigation if the material is obtained; and

b) to the circumstances under which the person in possession of the material holds it.

That material should be produced or access given to it but a production order would not be practicable because:
   - it is not practicable to communicate with any person entitled to produce the material; or
   - it is not practicable to communicate with any person entitled to grant access to the material or premises on which the material is situated; or
   - the investigation for which the application is made might be seriously prejudiced unless a constable arriving at the premises could secure immediate access to the material; or

continued on next page

Chapter 4 – Production Orders & Warrants

continued from previous page

a) that there are reasonable grounds for suspecting that a specified person has benefited from any criminal conduct; and

b) there are reasonable grounds for suspecting that there is on the premises any such material relating:
   - to the specified person, or
   - to the question whether that person has benefited from any criminal conduct or to any question as to the extent or whereabouts of the proceeds of any criminal conduct, and is likely to be of substantial value (whether by itself or together with other material) to the investigation for the purposes of which the application is made, but that the material cannot at the time of the application be particularised; and

c) that:
   - it is not practicable to communicate with any person entitled to grant entry to the premises; or
   - entry to the premises will not be granted unless a warrant is produced; or
   - the investigation for which the application is made might be seriously prejudiced unless a constable arriving at the premises could secure immediate entry to them; and

A constable entering premises in the execution of a warrant under this section, may seize and retain any material, other than items subject to legal privilege or excluded material, which is likely to be of substantial value to the investigation for which the warrant was issued.

See Appendix I for suggested format of application.

The orders and warrants in respect of the Drug Trafficking Act 1994 and the Criminal Justice Act 1988 require investigations into at least one of three areas:

- Whether a person has benefited.
- The extent of benefit.
- The whereabouts of benefit.

An investigation may fall into a permutation of one, two or three of the above areas. This investigation has to discover whether a person has benefited from crime or dealing in drugs. The whereabouts of benefit could be where a crime committed by a specified person is under investigation and the officer is now trying to locate the proceeds obtained by that crime. The word benefit under s71(4) and (5) Criminal Justice Act 1988 includes the value of any property or the sum equal to the value of any pecuniary advantage obtained by virtue of the crime. Where for instance the pecuniary advantage was the obtaining of a better employment by producing false references the benefit could be all the income obtained over whatever period that employment lasted. It will be the responsibility of future cases to define the concept of benefit. It is believed that Parliament intended benefit to have as wide an interpretation as possible in order to actually take away the profit from crime.

Applications under schedule 1 of the the Police and Criminal Evidence Act 1984 must be inter parte and therefore all interested parties informed of the application throughout the process. Where a production order for material under Police and Criminal Evidence Act 1984 is not complied with, this could never form the basis for an application for a warrant. There would need to be an action for contempt of court proceedings to force that party to produce the material. This is unlike the other Acts that use the failure to comply with a production order as the first ground for the issue of a production warrant.

Applications under the other legislation may all be held ex parte, the operative word here is *may*, officers should be ready to give reasons as to why the application should be heard ex parte. Without such reason a judge could consider that an inter parte application is more appropriate. Where an order or warrant granted ex parte is served or executed, the person on whom it is served or executed may apply to a court under the Crown Court Rules 1982 to discharge or vary such an order. The application would cause the judge to rule on the admissibility of materials obtained or sought under such an order.

The production orders all allow a judge to grant entry to premises in order to obtain access to the material, this is different to the power to force entry to premises under production warrants. It is therefore important that if the investigator needs to have immediate access to the person in control of the material, the order should contain the judge's authority for entry to premises.

The powers to force entry to premises with a production warrant are guided by the Codes of Practice. Code B para 5.12 indicates that premises must be secured before leaving, para 5.13 that an Inspector must be present and para 5.14 that the search is necessary to find property that is present.

Chapter 4 – Production Orders & Warrants

When entry is gained through a warrant any officer lawfully on premises may seize any material not subject to claims of legal privilege or excluded material that may be of substantial value to the investigation for which the warrant was issued. If during a search of premises, legal privilege is claimed against any material, it is not the investigator's prerogative to enter into any debate as to whether the material is or is not privileged material. If the investigator is suspicious about any claim of privilege the material could be placed in a sealed non-see-through bag in the presence of the person claiming privilege and taken to the Crown Prosecution Service for further advice. Section 19 of the Police and Criminal Evidence Act 1984 allows the seizure of any article connected with any offence in order to prevent loss, alteration, damage or destruction of the article.

Chapter 5
Specific Money Laundering Offences

Chapter 5
Specific Money Laundering Offences

You will remember there are three stages in the laundering cycle; placement – the initial stage is putting the money into a financial organisation, layering – is moving the money around the financial system in an effort to change its original identity, and finally integration – where the money is reintroduced as clean, free of any links with it's drug or crime origins.

Specific money laundering offences have been created to combat the laundering process at any of the three stages. The offences aim at making any person involved in the laundering cycle subject to the legislation. Offenders tempted to commit this type of offence subject themselves to a maximum term of imprisonment of 14 years.

The Criminal Justice Act 1988, as amended by the Criminal Justice Act 1993 and the Drug Trafficking Act 1994, created the specific money laundering offences. Chapter 2 looked at the Money Laundering Regulations 1993, the Criminal Justice Act 1993 and the Drug Trafficking Act 1994 which create offences around the three following specific areas:

- Assisting in the retaining of benefit of crime under s93A of the Criminal Justice Act 1993 and drugs under s50 of the Drug Trafficking Act 1994.

- Acquisition, possession or use of the direct or indirect proceeds of crime under s93B of the Criminal Justice Act 1993 and drugs under s51 of the Drug Trafficking Act 1994.

- Concealing or transferring of direct or indirect proceeds of crime under s93C of the Criminal Justice Act 1993 and drugs under s49 of the Drug Trafficking Act 1994.

The last point above relates to the criminal who conceals, disguises, converts or transfers property, with intent to avoid prosecution, or the enforcement of a confiscation order on any property which directly or indirectly represents his proceeds of crime or drugs. This offence is aimed at criminals themselves who make any attempt to launder their ill gotten gains. The remaining offences in the above points are aimed specifically at the criminals who play some part in knowingly laundering or arranging the laundering of a criminal's property.

The legislation impresses that persons who are suspicious about a drug or crime transaction should disclose their suspicions and thereby exempt themselves from prosecution or use the disclosure as a defence if prosecuted.

Set out in the rest of this chapter are the specific money laundering offences.

Assisting Another to Retain Benefit
Section 93A Criminal Justice Act 1988 as amended by Criminal Justice Act 1993 (commenced 15.2.94)
Where a person enters into or is otherwise concerned in an arrangement whereby:

- The retention or control by or on behalf of another's proceeds of criminal conduct is facilitated (whether by concealment, removal from jurisdiction, transfer to nominees or otherwise); or

- Proceeds of criminal conduct:
  - are used to secure funds placed at the others disposal; or
  - are used to benefit another to acquire property by way of investment, knowing or suspecting that the other is engaged in criminal conduct or has benefited from criminal conduct, he is guilty of an offence.

'Proceeds of criminal conduct' include any property which in whole or in part directly or indirectly represents his proceeds of criminal conduct. 'Criminal conduct' means conduct that constitutes an offence to which this Part of this Act applies or would constitute such an offence if it had occurred in England and Wales or Scotland.

Maximum Penalty
A person guilty of an offence under this section is liable summarily to 6 months' imprisonment, a fine to the statutory maximum or both. On indictment, 14 years' imprisonment, a fine or both.

Chapter 5 – Specific Money Laundering Offences

Defence
In proceedings it is a defence:

- That he did not know or suspect that the arrangement related to any person's proceeds of criminal conduct; or

- That he did not know or suspect that by the arrangement, the retention or control by or on behalf of another of any property was facilitated or, as the case may be, that by the arrangement any property was used in contravention of this section; or

- That he intended to disclose to a constable such a suspicion, belief or matter in relation to the arrangement, but there is a reasonable excuse for the failure to make a disclosure.

Where a person discloses to a constable the suspicion or belief that any funds or investments are derived from or used in connection with criminal conduct or discloses to a constable any matter on which such a suspicion or belief is based:

- The disclosure shall not be treated as a breach of any restriction upon the disclosure of information imposed by statute or otherwise; and

- If he does any act in contravention of this section and the disclosure relates to the arrangement concerned, he does not commit an offence under this section if:
  - the disclosure is made prior to the act concerned and the act is done with the consent of a constable; or
  - the disclosure is done, after an act on his initiative, and as soon as it is reasonable for him to make it.

Acquisition, Possession, or Use of Proceeds
Section 93B Criminal Justice Act 1988 as amended by Criminal Justice Act 1993 (commenced 15.2.94)
A person is guilty of an offence if, knowing that any property is, or in whole or in part directly or indirectly represents, another person's proceeds of criminal conduct, he acquires or uses that property or has possession of it. For the purpose of this section, having possession of any property shall be taken to be doing any act in relation to it. Providing of services or goods which are of assistance in criminal conduct shall not be treated as a consideration for the purposes of this section.

Maximum Penalty
A person guilty of an offence under this section is liable summarily to 6 months' imprisonment, a fine not exceeding the statutory maximum or both. On indictment, 14 years' imprisonment, a fine or both.

Defence
In proceedings it is a defence to prove the person charged acquired or used the property or had possession of it for adequate consideration.

In this section, having possession of any property shall be taken to be doing an act in relation to it; and a person acquires property for inadequate consideration if the value of the consideration is significantly less than the value of the property; and a person uses or has possession of property for inadequate consideration if the value of the consideration is significantly less than the value of his use or possession of the property. The provision for any person of services or goods which are of assistance to him in drug trafficking shall not be treated as consideration for the purposes of this section.

Where a person discloses to a constable a suspicion or belief that any property is, or in whole or in part directly or indirectly represents, another person's proceeds of drug trafficking, or discloses to a constable any matter on which such a suspicion or belief is based:

- The disclosure shall not be treated as a breach of any restriction upon the disclosure of information imposed by statute or otherwise; and
- If he does any act in relation to the property in contravention of this section, he does not commit an offence if:
  - the disclosure is made before he does the act concerned and the act is done with the consent of the constable; or
  - the disclosure is made after he does the act, but is made on his own initiative and as soon as it is reasonable for him to make it.

In proceedings for an offence under this section it is also a defence to prove:

- That he intended to disclose to a constable a suspicion, belief or matter as is mentioned in this section; but

Chapter 5 – Specific Money Laundering Offences

- There is a reasonable excuse for his failure to make the disclosure.

Persons in employment at the relevant time, will act in relation to disclosures and intended disclosures in compliance with the procedure established by employers for the making of such disclosures to a constable.

Concealing or Transferring Proceeds
Section 93C Criminal Justice Act 1988 as amended by Criminal Justice Act 1993 (commenced 15.2.94)
A person is guilty of an offence if he:

- Conceals or disguises any property which is, or in whole or in part, directly or indirectly represents, his proceeds of criminal conduct, or

- Converts or transfers that property or removes it from the jurisdiction, for the purpose of avoiding prosecution for an offence to which this Part of the Act applies or the making or enforcement in his case of a confiscation order.

A person is guilty of an offence if, knowing or having reasonable grounds to suspect that any property is, or in whole or in part directly or indirectly represents, another person's proceeds of criminal conduct he:

- Conceals or disguises that property, or

- Converts or transfers that property or removes it from the jurisdiction, for the purpose of assisting any person to avoid prosecution for an offence to which Part of this Act applies or the making or enforcement in his case of a confiscation order.

Maximum Penalty
A person guilty of an offence under this section is liable summarily to 6 months' imprisonment, a fine to the statutory maximum or both. On indictment, 14 years' imprisonment, a fine or both.

References to concealing or disguising any property include references to concealing or disguising it's nature, source, location, disposition, movement or ownership, or any rights with respect to it.

Note: A constable or other person shall not be guilty of an offence in respect of anything done in the course of acting in connection with enforcement or intended enforcement of any provision of this Act or of any other enactment relating to criminal conduct or the proceeds of such conduct.

Concealing or Transferring Own Proceeds of Drug Trafficking
Section 49(1) Drug Trafficking Act 1994
A person is guilty of offence if he:

- Conceals or disguises any property which is, or in whole or in part directly or indirectly represents, his proceeds of drug trafficking; or converts; or transfers that property; or removes it from the jurisdiction.

- For the purpose of avoiding prosecution of himself for a drug trafficking offence or enforcement in his case of a confiscation order.

By s49(3) concealing or disguising any property includes concealing or disguising its nature, source, location, disposition, movement, or ownership or any right in respect of such property.

Concealing or Transferring Another's Proceeds of Drug Trafficking
Section 49(2) Drug Trafficking Act 1994
A person is guilty of an offence if he:

- Knowing or having reasonable grounds to suspect that any property is, or in whole or in part directly or indirectly represents, another person's proceeds of drug trafficking.

- Conceals or disguises that property; or converts or transfers that property; or removes it from the jurisdiction. For the purpose of assisting any person to avoid prosecution for a drug trafficking offence or the making of an enforcement or confiscation order.

Maximum Penalty
A person guilty of an offence under ss49, 50 or 51 of the Drug Trafficking Act 1994 shall be liable summarily to 6 months'

Chapter 5 – Specific Money Laundering Offences

imprisonment, a fine to the statutory maximum or both. On indictment, to a term not exceeding 14 years' imprisonment, a fine or both.

Assisting Another Person to Retain the Benefit of Drug Trafficking
Section 50 Drug Trafficking Act 1994

A person is guilty of an offence if he enters into or is otherwise concerned in an arrangement whereby:

- The retention or control by or on behalf of another person (call him 'A') of A's proceeds of drug trafficking is facilitated (whether by concealment, removal from the jurisdiction, transfer to nominees or otherwise); or
- A's proceeds of drug trafficking:
  - are used to secure that funds are placed at A's disposal, or
  - are used for A's benefit to acquire property by way of investment, and he knows or suspects that A is a person who carries on or has carried on drug trafficking or has benefited from drug trafficking.

In this section, references to any person's proceeds of drug trafficking include a reference to any property which is, or in whole or in part directly or indirectly represents, his proceeds of drug trafficking.

Where a person discloses to a constable a suspicion or belief that any funds or investments are derived from or used in connection with drug trafficking, or discloses to a constable any matter on which such a suspicion or belief is based:

- The disclosure shall not be treated as a breach of any restriction upon the disclosure of information imposed by statute or otherwise; and
- If he does any act in contravention of this section and the disclosure relates to the arrangement concerned, he does not commit an offence under this section if:
  - the disclosure is made before he does the act concerned and the act is done with the consent of the constable; or
  - the disclosure is made after he does the act, but is made on his own initiative and as soon as it is reasonable for him to make it.

Defence
In proceedings for an offence under this section, it is a defence to prove:

- That he did not know or suspect that the arrangement related to any person's proceeds of drug trafficking; or
- That it would secure funds or investments or facilitate such an act as set out in the offence; or
- That he intended to disclose to a constable such a suspicion, belief or matter as is mentioned in the section above in relation to the arrangement, but there is a reasonable excuse for the failure to make any such disclosure.

In the case of a person who was in employment at the time in question, disclosures, and intended disclosures, may be made to the appropriate person in accordance with the procedure established by his employer for the making of such disclosures as they have effect in relation to disclosures, and intended disclosures, to a constable.

Acquisition, Possession or Use of Drug Trafficking
Section 51 Drug Trafficking Act 1994
A person is guilty of an offence if:

- Knowing that any property is, or in whole or in part directly or indirectly represents, another person's proceeds of drug trafficking, he acquires or uses that property or has possession of it.

Defence
It is a defence to an offence under this section:

- That the person charged acquired or used the property or had possession of it for adequate consideration.
- In this section, having possession of any property shall be taken to be doing an act in relation to it, and a person acquires property for inadequate consideration if the value of the consideration is significantly less than the value of the property; and a person uses or has possession of property for inadequate consideration if the value of the consideration is significantly less than the value of his use or possession of the property. The provision for any

Chapter 5 – Specific Money Laundering Offences

person of services or goods which are of assistance to him in drug trafficking shall not be treated as consideration for the purposes of this section.

In proceedings for an offence under this section, it is a defence to prove that:

- He intended to disclose to a constable such a suspicion, belief or matter as is mentioned in this section, but
- There is reasonable excuse for his failure to make any such disclosure.

Where a person discloses to a constable a suspicion or belief that any property is, or in whole or in part directly or indirectly represents, another person's proceeds of drug trafficking, or discloses to a constable any matter on which such a suspicion or belief is based:

- The disclosure shall not be treated as a breach of any restriction upon the disclosure of information imposed by statute or otherwise; and
- If he does any act in relation to the property in contravention of this section, he does not commit an offence if:
  - the disclosure is made before he does the act concerned and the act is done with the consent of the constable; or
  - the disclosure is made after he does the act, but is made on his own initiative and as soon as it is reasonable for him to make it.

In the case of a person who was in employment at the time in question, disclosures, and intended disclosures, may be made to the appropriate person in accordance with the procedure established by his employer.

No constable or other person shall be guilty of an offence under this section in respect of anything done by him in the course of acting in connection with the enforcement, or intended enforcement, of any provision of this Act or of any other enactment relating to drug trafficking or the proceeds of drug trafficking.

Powers to Seize Drug Monies

In addition to the legislation to prevent money laundering the legislators realised that drugs, particularly the more addictive kinds, are grown and manufactured outside the UK. Some of the ingredients for manufacture of some drugs are more easily purchased outside the UK. In order to make such illicit drug transactions, the drug suppliers have to get money into other jurisdictions by using couriers to convey large amounts of cash. The UK was also a rich source and attractive market for overseas drug cartels to launder their proceeds again by the use of couriers conveying cash across borders into the UK. In order to combat this traffic in drug money initially powers to seize such monies were put in place by s25 of the Criminal Justice (International Co-operation) Act 1990. No offence is created within this section, merely powers to seize and detain monies whilst a decision is made as to their origins and or the prosecution of the couriers or application for the forfeiture of the monies.

The Drug Trafficking Act 1994 now includes s42 that empowers a constable or customs officer to seize and detain drug monies amounting to £10,000 (or the equivalent) or above (*see below*). The cash so seized may result in the prosecution of the courier for one of the preceding money laundering offences, and could result in an application, under the civil burden of proof, for the monies to be forfeited. The section allows any party to the application, except the applicant, to apply to the court to allow part of the monies to be released to meet legal expenses incurred in any application or appeal to the Crown Courts.

All monies seized or detained under this section unless actually bearing forensic, fingerprint, or other evidence must be paid into an interest-bearing account. The seizure application and any orders should reflect not only the original cash but include any interest that may have accrued on the cash.

Let us now examine this legislation.

Seizure and Detention of Cash
Section 42 Drug Trafficking Act 1994
A customs officer or constable may seize and detain cash being imported into or exported from the United Kingdom providing:

Chapter 5 – Specific Money Laundering Offences

- The amount is not less than the prescribed sum (currently £10,000); and
- There are reasonable grounds to suspect that it directly or indirectly represents any persons proceeds of, or is intended by any person, for use in drug trafficking.

Cash seized may only be detained for 48 hours unless further detention order is granted by JP or Scottish Sheriff, an order will only be granted if:

- There are reasonable grounds to suspect that it directly or indirectly represents any persons proceeds or is intended by any person, for use in drug trafficking; and
- Satisfied that continued detention is justified while its origin or derivation is further investigated; or
- Consideration is given to the institution of criminal proceedings against any person for an offence with which the cash is connected; and
- Court may authorise continued detention of cash for periods not exceeding 3 months up to maximum of 2 years from date of first order.

Notice to be given to persons affected by the order.

Cash seized and detained for more than 48 hours (unless required as evidence) must be held in an interest-bearing account, and any interest accrued added to any order made or its total if restored, upon satisfactory explanation.

At any time while cash is detained, a magistrates' court or Sheriff may direct its release if satisfied:

- On application by person from whom it was seized or person on whose behalf it was being imported or exported or any other person that there are no longer justified grounds for detention; or
- A customs officer or constable, or procurator fiscal in Scotland, may release the cash if satisfied detention is no longer justified but must first notify the court or person under whose order it is detained; or
- Under s43, on application of constable, Commissioner of

Customs & Excise or Procurator Fiscal, a magistrates' court or Sheriff may order the forfeiture of the cash and accrued interest providing, on a civil standard of proof, they are satisfied the cash represents any person's proceeds of drug trafficking.

Tipping Off

Parliament realised that during a financial investigation it was inevitable that a number of people could discover that an inquiry was being conducted. In an attempt to preserve the integrity of such an investigation 'tipping off' offences were created. In order to prevent the disclosure of sensitive information to the suspect parties both the Criminal Justice Act 1988 and the Drug Trafficking Act 1994 contain offences in respect of 'tipping off'.

The offence is in three parts:

- Where a constable is conducting an investigation into money laundering.
- Where a constable is conducting investigations into a disclosure.
- Where a disclosure has been made to any person.

Defence
In proceedings under either Act it is a defence to prove that the person did not know or suspect that the disclosure or investigation could be prejudiced.

Section 93D Criminal Justice Act 1988 as amended by Criminal Justice Act 1993 (commenced 1.4.94)

A person is guilty of an offence if:

- He knows or suspects that a constable is acting, or is proposing to act, in connection with an investigation which is being or is about to be conducted into money laundering; and
- He discloses to any other person information or any other matter which is likely to prejudice that investigation or proposed investigation; or

Chapter 5 – Specific Money Laundering Offences

- He knows or suspects that a disclosure has been made to a constable under s93A or 93B; and
- He discloses to another information or any other matter which is likely to prejudice any investigation which may be conducted following the disclosure or proposed investigation; or
- He knows or suspects a disclosure under s93A or 93B has been made to any person; and
- He discloses to any person information or any other matter which is likely to prejudice any investigation which might be conducted following the disclosure.

Maximum Penalty

A person guilty of an offence under this section shall be liable summarily to 6 months' imprisonment, a fine to the statutory maximum or both. On indictment 5 years' imprisonment, a fine or both.

A professional legal adviser is exempt when disclosing information to a representative of, or a client in connection with, the giving or receiving of legal advice, or to any person in contemplation of or in connection with legal proceedings for the purpose of those proceedings.

This section does not apply in the furtherance of a criminal purpose as defined under s10(2) PACE 1984.

A constable or other person shall not be guilty of an offence in respect of anything done in the course of acting in connection with enforcement or intended enforcement of any provision of this Act or of any other enactment relating to criminal conduct or the proceeds of such conduct.

In this section 'money laundering' means doing any act that constitutes an offence under s93A, 93B, or 93C above or, in the case of an act committed otherwise than in England and Wales or Scotland, would constitute an offence if committed in England and Wales or Scotland. Having possession of any property shall be taken to be doing an act in relation to it.

Section 53 Drug Trafficking Act 1994
A person is guilty of an offence if:

- He knows or suspects that a constable is acting, or is proposing to act, in connection with an investigation which is being or is about to be conducted into drug money laundering; and

  He discloses to any other person information or any other matter which is likely to prejudice any investigation or proposed investigation.

- He knows or suspects that a disclosure has been made to a constable under s50, 51 or 52 of this Act; and

  He discloses to another information or any other matter which is likely to prejudice any investigation which may be conducted following the disclosure.

- He knows or suspects a disclosure has been made to any person; and

  He discloses to any person information or any other matter which is likely to prejudice any investigation which might be conducted following the disclosure.

Maximum Penalty
A person guilty of an offence under this section shall be liable summarily to 6 months' imprisonment, a fine to the statutory maximum or both. On indictment, 5 years' imprisonment, a fine or both.

A professional legal adviser is exempt when disclosing information to a representative of, or a client in connection with, the giving or receiving of legal advice, or to any person in contemplation of or in connection with legal proceedings for the purpose of those proceedings. This section does not apply in the furtherance of a criminal purpose as defined in s10(2) PACE 1984.

A constable or other person shall not be guilty of an offence under this section in respect of anything done in the course of acting in connection with enforcement or intended enforcement of any provision of this Act or of any other enactment relating to drug trafficking or the proceeds of drug trafficking.

Chapter 5 – Specific Money Laundering Offences

Money Laundering

Financial Assistance for Terrorism
Section 9 Part III of the Prevention of Terrorism (Temporary Provisions) Act 1989
A person is guilty of an offence if he:

- Solicits or invites any other person to give, lend or otherwise make available, whether for a consideration or not, any money or other property; or

  Receives or accepts from any other person, whether for consideration or not, any money or other property, intending that it shall be applied or used for the commission of, or in furtherance of or in connection with acts of terrorism to which this section applies or having reasonable cause to suspect that it may be so used or applied.

- Gives, lends or otherwise make available to any other person, whether for consideration or not, any money or other property; or

  Enters into or is otherwise concerned in an arrangement whereby money or other property is or is to be made available to another person, knowing or having reasonable cause to suspect that it will or may be applied or used for the commission of, or in furtherance of or in connection with acts of terrorism to which this section applies or having reasonable cause to suspect that it may be so used or applied.

The acts of terrorism to which this section applies are:

- Acts of terrorism connected with the affairs of Northern Ireland; and
- Any other acts of terrorism of any other description which if committed in the UK would be triable in the UK except acts which are solely connected with the affairs of any part of the UK other than Northern Ireland.

Defence
In relation to acts committed outside the UK the prosecution need to prove that the person knew or had reasonable cause to

suspect the act would constitute an offence of the nature triable within the UK but it is for the defence to prove that he did not know or suspect that the offence constituted such an offence.

The court dealing with a person under s9(1) or (2) may order under s13(2) and (3) the forfeiture of monies or other property to which the offences related.

Obtaining Contributions to Resources of Proscribed Organisations
Section 10 Part III of the Prevention of Terrorism (Temporary Provisions) Act 1989
A person is guilty of an offence if he:

- Solicits or invites any other person to give, lend, or otherwise make available, whether for consideration or not, any money or other property for the benefit of a proscribed organisation; or
- Gives, lends, or otherwise make available or receives or accepts, whether for consideration or not, any money or other property for the benefit of such organisation; or
- Enters into or is otherwise concerned in an arrangement whereby money or other property is or is to be made available for the benefit of such organisation.

Defence
In proceedings under this section it is a defence to prove:

- The defendant did not know and had no reasonable cause to suspect that the money was for the benefit of a proscribed organisation and for the defence to prove that he did not know or reasonably suspect that the transaction related to a proscribed organisation.

The court dealing with a person under s10(1)(a) or (b) may order under s13(4) the forfeiture of monies or other property to which the offences related.

Note: There are no facilities under the Act to proscribe any organisation other than those connected with Northern Ireland, but the Act includes that organisations proscribed under the Northern Ireland (Emergency Provisions) Act 1978 relate purely to Northern Ireland.

Chapter 5 – Specific Money Laundering Offences

Assisting in Retention or Control of Funds
Section 11 Part III of the Prevention of Terrorism (Temporary Provisions) Act 1989
A person is guilty of an offence if he:

- Enters into or is otherwise concerned in an arrangement whereby the retention or control by or on behalf of another person of terrorist funds is facilitated, whether by concealment, removal from the jurisdiction, transfer to nominees or otherwise.

Defence
In proceedings under this section it is a defence to prove:

- The defendant did not know and had no reasonable cause to suspect that the arrangement related to terrorist funds.

Terrorist funds means funds that may be applied or used in the commission of or in furtherance of or connection with offences specified in s9, or the proceeds of such acts or activities in furtherance of or in connection with such acts, or the resources of proscribed organisations.

The court dealing with a person under s11 may order under s13(3) the forfeiture of monies or other property to which the offences related.

Maximum Penalty
A person guilty of an offence under s9, 10 or 11 is liable on indictment to 14 years' imprisonment, a fine or both. Summarily to 6 months' imprisonment, a fine not exceeding the statutory maximum or both.

Disclosure of Information
Section 12 Part III Prevention of Terrorism (Temporary Provisions) Act 1989

A person may notwithstanding any restriction on the disclosure of information imposed by contract disclose to a constable a suspicion or belief that money or other property is derived from terrorist funds or any matter on which such suspicion is based.

A person who enters into or is concerned in an offence contrary to s9, 10 or 11 does not commit an offence if:

- He is acting with the express consent of a constable; or
- He discloses to a constable his suspicion or belief that money or other property is derived from terrorist funds or any matter on which such suspicion is based; and
- The disclosure is made after he enters into or becomes concerned in the transaction but is made on his own initiative and as soon as is practicable for him to make it.

Note: The above does not apply when expressly forbidden by a constable to undertake such transactions.

Defence
It is a defence in proceedings to prove:

- That he intended to disclose to a constable his suspicions or belief; and
- That there is a reasonable excuse for his failure to disclose such information.

Chapter 6
Restraint & Charging Orders

Chapter 6
Restraint & Charging Orders

Restraint Orders

The purpose of a restraint order is to prevent the person against whom an order is made, from dissipating or disposing of assets that may in the fullness of time be used to satisfy a confiscation order. Restraint orders can therefore only be obtained where there are grounds for believing at the time of the application that a confiscation order will be made in respect of realisable property. There is no power to obtain restraint on any property which may be forfeited, or form the subject of a compensation order or a fine.

A restraint order can be made in respect of all property in the control of a particular person. The orders are against a named party, not the property, they prevent the party from dealing in any way with property, without leave of the court or as mentioned in conditions attached to such orders. Where the order is of a general nature against a defendant it must include provision for payment of legal expenses (*Customs and Excise Commissioners v Norris* (1991)) and may include a provision for living expenses. This or any part of the order may be varied by application of any party to the order, or consent of the parties to the order. Restraint orders must be discharged at the conclusion of the proceedings to which they relate.

Applications for restraint orders are made through the High Court in London by a prosecutor using a sworn affidavit of a police officer involved in the financial investigations of the defendant. The affidavit must contain all the information available in respect of the subject property whether it is favourable or unfavourable to the prosecution. The Central Confiscation Branch of the Crown Prosecution Service will advise on the content required for such an affidavit. The Criminal Justice Act 1988, as amended by the Proceeds of Crime Act 1995, applies to cases after 1st November 1995 and does not specify a minimum amount for restraint orders, leaving the decision as to proceedings with the prosecution. The costs of any applications are only recoverable from available monies, therefore applications will generally be made in cases over £10,000 otherwise the costs could outweigh the benefits. The Criminal Justice Act 1988, in force prior to 1st November 1995, enforces a £10,000 minimum for confiscation and restraint cases. The Drug Trafficking Act 1994 commenced on 3rd February 1995 and no set figure is contained in the legislation, pursuance of restraint orders is a matter for the prosecution. Restraint orders are served personally on the defendant and a notice of the order must be given to all interested parties. In practice financial institutions will accept faxed copies followed by the original delivered by recorded post or by hand.

In the course of a High Court application a person can be ordered to disclose details of all their realisable property, but remember any information so obtained cannot be used in criminal proceedings against a defendant or spouse (*Re C (Restraint Orders Identification)* (1995)). Where the High Court has granted a restraint order that court may order the person concerned to relocate assets to within the jurisdiction of the High Court, this is known as repatriation.

The High Court has powers to order the disclosure of information held by a Government Department for the purposes of facilitating restraint, charging orders, or the realisation of property. Those powers can be found under the following Acts and sections:

- Section 93J of the Criminal Justice Act 1988, as amended by Proceeds of Crime Act 1995.
- Section 59 of the Drug Trafficking Act 1994.

Breach of the restraint order is contempt of the High Court and can be punished with a fine or imprisonment or both until such time as the contempt is purged. The Central Confiscation Branch will deal and advise in all applications for restraint orders and should be contacted as early as possible.

Restraint orders are obtained under the following Acts and sections:

- Sections 76 and 77 of the Criminal Justice Act 1988, as amended by the Proceeds of Crime Act 1995.
- Sections 25 and 26 of the Drug Trafficking Act 1994.

Chapter 6 – Restraint & Charging Orders

- Schedule 4 of the Prevention of Terrorism (Temporary Provisions) Act 1989.

Those sections are portrayed separately as follows.

Section 26 Drug Trafficking Act 1994
The High Court may issue a restraint order prohibiting any person from dealing with any realisable property, subject to conditions and exceptions as specified by the order. A restraint order may make any provision as the court thinks fit for legal or living expenses.

For the purposes of this section, dealing with property held by any person includes:

- Where a debt is owed to that person, making a payment to any person in reduction of the amount of the debt; and
- Removing the property from Great Britain.

Section 25 Drug Trafficking Act 1994
Restraint orders may be made by the High Court when:

- Proceedings have been instituted in England and Wales against the defendant for a s1 drug trafficking offence; or
- Prosecutor has applied against the defendant under any of following sections:
    - s13 – Reconsideration of new evidence
    - s14 – Re-assessment of benefit
    - s15 – Revised proceeds
    - s16 – Increased realisable property
    - s19 – High Court powers regarding dead or disappeared defendant; or
- Court is satisfied that:
    - by the laying of an information or otherwise, a person is to be charged with a s1 drug trafficking offence or that an application under s13, 14, 15, 16, or 19 mentioned above, is to be made in respect of the defendant; and
- The court has reasonable cause to believe:
    - In an application under s15 (revision of proceeds) that the court will make a fresh determination as in s15(4).

- In an application under s16 (increased realisable property) that the court will make an increase in the realisable property order as in s16(2); or
- In any other case, that the defendant has benefited from drug trafficking and the proceedings have not, or the application has not, been concluded.

The court shall not make a restraint order when:

- There has been undue delay in continuing the proceedings or the application in question; or
- The prosecutor does not intend to proceed with a prosecution or any application in respect of such property.

Section 77 Criminal Justice Act 1988

A restraint order:

- May be made only on an application by the prosecutor.
- May be made on an ex parte application to a judge in Chambers; and shall provide for notice to be given to all parties affected by the order.
- May apply to all realisable property held by a specified person, whether the property is described in the order or not; and
- To all realisable property held by a specified person, even property transferred to their possession after the making of the order; and
- May be discharged or varied in relation to any property.
- Shall be discharged on the conclusion of the proceedings or on the application in question.
- Any person affected may apply for the discharge or variation of a restraint order.
- Shall not have effect in relation to any property being subject to a charging order under s27 of this Act or s9 of the Drug Trafficking Offences Act 1986.

The High Court may issue a restraint order prohibiting any person from dealing with any realisable property, subject to any conditions or exceptions specified by the order. A restraint order

Chapter 6 – Restraint & Charging Orders

may make provision as the court thinks fit for living or legal expenses.

For the purposes of this section, dealing with the property held by any person includes:

- Where a debt is owed to that person, making a payment to any other person to reduce the amount of the debt; and
- Removing property from Great Britain.

Restraint orders cannot be made in respect of any property subject of a charging order under s78.

Where the High Court has made a restraint order, a High Court or a County Court:

- May at any time appoint a receiver:
  - to take possession of any realisable property, and
  - in accordance with the court's directions, to manage or otherwise deal with any property in respect of which he is appointed, subject to such exceptions and conditions as may be specified by the court; and
- May require any person having possession of property in respect of which a receiver is appointed under this section to give possession of it to the receiver; and
- A constable may seize any realisable property for the purpose of preventing its removal from Great Britain, and will act under the court's directions in respect of such property.

Section 76 Criminal Justice Act 1988

Restraint orders may be made by the High Court when:

- Proceedings have been instituted in England and Wales against any person for an offence to which this Act applies; or
- Prosecutor has applied against the defendant under any of following sections:
  - s74A – Revised proceeds
  - s74B – Re-assessment of benefit
  - s74C – Increased realisable property; or
- The court is satisfied that, by the laying of an information

or otherwise, a person is to be charged with an offence to which this Act applies or that an application under s74A, 74B or 74C mentioned above, is to be made in respect of the defendant.

And the court has reasonable cause to believe:

- In an application under s74C (increased realisable property) that the court will make a fresh determination as in s74C(3); or
- In any other case, that the defendant has benefited from an offence of a relevant description and proceedings may or have resulted in a conviction or reference is made to the previous conviction and the proceedings have not, or the application has not, been concluded.

The High Court shall not make a restraint order when:

- There has been undue delay in the proceedings, or application; or
- That the person making the application, appears to the court, likely to fail to proceed with the application; and
- The High Court shall discharge the order if proceedings in respect of the offence are not instituted or no application is made within a reasonable time.

A restraint order:

- May be made only on an application by the prosecutor.
- May be made on an ex parte application to a judge in Chambers and shall provide for a notice to be given to all parties affected by the order.
- May be discharged or varied at any time in relation to any property.
- Will automatically be discharged when proceedings are concluded by the making of a forfeiture order or there is no possibility of such an order being made.
- May be discharged or varied on the application of any person affected by the order.
- May be made in respect of registered land and a caution

can be placed on such land inhibiting any dealing in such land without consent of the High Court.

- May apply to all realisable property held by a specified person, whether the property is described in the order or not; and
- To all realisable property held by a specified person, even property transferred to their possession after the making of the order; and
- May be discharged or varied in relation to any property.
- Shall be discharged on the conclusion of the proceedings or of the application in question.

Where the High Court has made a restraint order:

- A constable may seize property to prevent its removal from the jurisdiction of the High Court and will act under the court's direction in respect of such property.
- The court may discharge the order where proceedings are not instituted within a reasonable time. (Note: proceedings include summons, warrant, or charge without warrant.)

The court may appoint a receiver:

- To take possession of any realisable property; and
- In accordance with the court's directions, to manage or otherwise deal with any property in respect of which he is appointed, subject to exceptions or conditions specified by the court. The receiver may require any person in possession of property in respect of which a receiver is appointed to give possession of it to the receiver.

Schedule 4 Prevention of Terrorism (Temporary Provisions) Act 1989

Restraint orders may be made by the High Court when:

- Proceedings have been instituted for a Part III offence and have not been concluded; or
- A forfeiture order has been made or reasonable grounds exist to expect a court to make such an order; or

- The High Court is satisfied by a complaint or otherwise that a person is to be charged with a Part III offence; and
- A forfeiture order may be made in such proceedings.

The restraint order will prohibit any person from dealing with any property in respect of which a forfeiture order has or may be made. This includes payment in reduction of a debt to a third party, or removing the property from the jurisdiction of the High Court.

A restraint order:

- May be made only by the application of the prosecution and may be made on an ex parte application to a judge in Chambers.
- Shall ensure that a notice is given to all parties affected by the order.
- May be discharged or varied at any time in relation to any property.
- Will automatically be discharged when proceedings are concluded by the making of a forfeiture order or there is no possibility of such an order being made.
- May be discharged or varied on the application of any person affected by the order.
- May be made in respect of registered land and a caution can be placed on such land inhibiting any dealing in such land without consent of the High Court.

Where the court have made a restraint order:

- A constable may seize property to prevent the removal from the court's jurisdiction and will act under the court's direction in respect of such property.
- The court may discharge the order where proceedings are not instituted within a reasonable time. (Note: proceedings include summons, warrant, or charge without warrant.)
- The court may appoint a receiver:
  - to take possession of any realisable property, and in accordance with the court's directions, to manage or

otherwise deal with any property in respect of which he is appointed, subject to such exceptions and conditions as may be specified by the court; and
- may require any person having possession of property in respect of which a receiver is appointed under this section to give possession of it to the receiver.

The Prevention of Terrorism Act 1989 allows for the making of restraint orders in England and Wales, Scotland, and Northern Ireland. The orders in Northern Ireland are obtainable in the same way as those obtained in England and Wales but the definition of proceedings for an offence include when an indictment is presented under s2(2)(c) of the Grand Jury (Abolition) Act 1969. Scottish restraint orders have similar conditions to those obtainable in England and Wales, but they are obtainable by application to the Court of Sessions by the Lord Advocate.

Charging Orders

Charging orders are High Court orders made against specified realisable property in order to secure the payment of money to the Crown. These orders can only be made in respect of land registered in England or Wales; securities held in UK government stock, any other stock in bodies incorporated within England and Wales or stock from other countries that hold a register of such in England and Wales; and unit trusts registered in England and Wales. The charges are registered with the body having responsibility for maintaining such registers, for example, the Land Registry or Companies House. The Acts allow for not only a charge against the stocks, securities and unit trusts but may extend to any interest or dividends that are payable from such an interest, for example, annual dividends payable on stocks.

There are conditions on the obtaining of charging orders, similar to those relating to restraint orders. The orders can be obtained prior to a confiscation order being made and in that case are limited to the value of the property charged, or after a confiscation order is obtained to an amount equal to the order. The orders can contain conditions which the court thinks fit and must be discharged when the confiscation order has been met even if the order is met from other funds. The court may make an order varying or discharging the charging order at any time on the application of any person affected by the order.

Charging orders are obtainable under the following sections:

- Section 27 of the Drug Trafficking Act 1994.
- Section 78 of the Criminal Justice Act 1988.

The High Court has powers, which are only available on the application of a prosecutor, to order the disclosure of information held by a Government Department for the purposes of facilitating charging orders. These powers can be found under the following Acts and sections:

- Section 93J of the Criminal Justice Act 1988, as amended by the Proceeds of Crime Act 1995.
- Section 59 of the Drug Trafficking Act 1994.

Section 78 Criminal Justice Act 1988 and Section 27 Drug Trafficking Act 1994

The High Court may make a charging order on realisable property for securing the payment to the Crown:

- Where a confiscation order has not been made, of an amount equal to the value from time to time of the property charged; and
- In any case, of an amount not exceeding the amount payable under the confiscation order.

Realisable property on which charging orders can be made includes:

- Land in England and Wales; or
- Securities of any of the following kinds:
  - government stock
  - stock of any body incorporated in England and Wales
  - stock of any body incorporated outside England and Wales where the register is kept within England and Wales
  - units of any unit trust of which a register is kept within England and Wales.

Chapter 6 – Restraint & Charging Orders

A charging order:

- May be made only on an application by the prosecutor and such application may be made by an ex parte application to a judge in Chambers.
- Shall provide for a notice to be given to all persons affected by the order.
- May be made subject to such conditions as the court thinks fit, including such conditions as it thinks fit as to the time when the charge is to become effective.

Such a charge may be imposed by a charging order only on:

- Any interest in realisable property, being an interest held beneficially by the defendant or by a person to whom the defendant has directly or indirectly made a gift caught by this Part of this Act:
  - in any asset of a kind mentioned above; or
  - under any trust; or
- Any interest in realisable property held by a person as trustee of a trust if the interest is in such an asset, or is an interest under another trust and a charge may by virtue of the first point above be imposed by a charging order on the whole beneficial interest under the first mentioned trust.

Where a court has made a charging order, the court:

- May on the application of any person affected by the order, at any time, make an order discharging or varying it; and
- Shall make an order discharging it on the occurrence of whichever of the following first occurs:
  - the conclusion of the proceedings or the application in question, or
  - the payment into court of the full amount, payment of which is secured by the charge.

Chapter 7
Confiscation Orders

Chapter 7
Confiscation Orders

The unwritten principle of English law is that no person shall profit by criminal conduct. This forms the basis of confiscation legislation which has been drafted to deprive defendants of their benefit from crime and illicit drugs. The legislation is divided into two distinctive headings – forfeiture and confiscation. In this chapter we will examine the legislation appertaining to confiscation and confiscation orders, Chapter 8 will deal with forfeiture.

Confiscation orders should not be confused with a forfeiture order, the latter is an order which transfers title from the defendant to the Crown, a confiscation order is an order to pay a sum of money, stated in sterling, to the Crown. The court cannot specify how the defendant will dispose of assets in order to pay the specified sum nor may it pass title of assets to the state. The Prevention of Terrorism (Temporary Provisions) Act 1989 contains no section relating to confiscation and only allows forfeiture orders.

Confiscation orders are orders of a court to confiscate the benefit obtained by virtue of an offence to which the relevant Acts relate. In order to make a confiscation order the court will require the prosecutor to furnish it with a statement known as a 'prosecutor's statement' (*see Appendix II*). This statement contains details of the benefit derived from the crime including any assumptions made in respect of such calculations including details of all realisable property and other assets, including gifts to other people, available for confiscation

The standard for proving the defendant's benefit for a confiscation order is the civil standard of proof, which is, 'the balance of probabilities'. This applies to all cases under the Drug Trafficking Act 1994 and the Criminal Justice Act 1988, after 3rd February 1995. Cases that commenced under both Acts prior to 3rd February 1995 require the criminal standard of proof, which is, 'beyond reasonable doubt'. There should be very few such cases left in the criminal justice system.

Confiscation orders consider two distinct sums:

- The total value of benefit; and
- The total value of realisable property.

Section 71 of the Criminal Justice Act 1988, as amended by the Criminal Justice Act 1993 and the Proceeds of Crime Act 1995, states that a person benefits from an offence if he obtains property as a result of or in connection with its commission and his benefit is the value of the property so obtained. If a person derives a pecuniary advantage as a result of or in connection with an offence then he is to be treated for the purposes of this Part of the Act as if he had obtained a sum equal to the value of the pecuniary advantage.

Section 74 of the Criminal Justice Act 1988, as amended, and s6(2) of the Drug Trafficking Act 1994 states property is not property if:

- A deprivation order is in force.
- A forfeiture order is in force.
- A Scottish forfeiture order is in force.

Therefore a confiscation order cannot be made in respect of benefit that is subject to any of the aforementioned orders.

In order to inform a court of the details of benefit or realisable property, the definition of property has to be understood. Property is defined by s4 of the Theft Act 1968 as money and all other property, real or personal, including things in action and other intangible property. Section 10 of the Criminal Damage Act 1971 provides the definition that property includes all property real, tangible, and personal and adds wild creatures tamed or kept in captivity and any wild creatures or their carcasses that have been reduced into possession not including wild plants, fungus, fruit or foliage growing wild. The more unusual items are met infrequently, but the investigator needs an awareness of items that are easily purchased, easily hidden, openly accepted and quickly sold to launder tainted monies. These may include personalised car registration numbers, stamp or philatelic collections, rare birds or animals, rare carpets, paintings, stocks, bonds, shares and even legally-enforceable debts.

Chapter 7 – Confiscation Orders

In order to ascertain the value of benefit or the realisable value of property, a court will hold a hearing to determine these values. This is known as a determination hearing. The hearing is held after conviction. The hearing may be held after a postponement, or prior to or after sentencing, but in most cases will form part of the sentencing hearing. The grounds for a hearing, or the postponement, are dealt with separately within this chapter.

The court cannot make an order in a sum of more than the value of realisable property as defined by s74 of the Criminal Justice Act 1988, as amended, and s6(2) of the Drug Trafficking Act 1994. 'Realisable property' is defined as any property held by the defendant and any property held by a person to whom the defendant has directly or indirectly made a gift as defined by the Act.

The court having made an order for the value of realisable property may reduce that amount where the defendant makes application that the property did not realise such an amount, again the civil standard of proof applies to the defendant's application. In order to make such an application the defendant may apply to the High Court for a certificate of inadequacy that is then used to apply to the Crown Court for a variation of the confiscation order. In addition, the Crown Court on application of the prosecutor, can in certain circumstances revise the confiscation order or when the original court was misled make a new order. This revision of orders will be covered in more detail towards the end of this chapter.

Compensation, where victims of crime are identified, may be ordered through the confiscation order and the sums paid to the court will be used to first satisfy the compensation and then the confiscation part of the order. Where an order for confiscation and compensation is made against the same person in the same proceedings, and it appears that there will not be sufficient means to satisfy both orders in full, the court shall direct that the compensation will be met from the funds available for confiscation.

Confiscation orders are made under the following sections:

- Crime – Section 71 of the Criminal Justice Act 1988, as amended by the Criminal Justice Act 1993 and the Proceeds of Crime Act 1995.
- Drugs – Section 2 of the Drug Trafficking Act 1994.

The powers to make confiscation orders are broken down as follows:

Section 71 Criminal Justice Act 1988 as amended by Criminal Justice Act 1993 and Proceeds of Crime Act 1995

Where an offender is convicted, in proceedings before the Crown Court of an indictable offence (**not** a drug trafficking offence), or at a magistrates' court, of an offence listed in Schedule IV of this Act, it shall be the duty of the court where:

- The prosecutor gives written notice to the court that it would be appropriate for the court to proceed under this section; or
- The court considers, even though it has not been given such notice, that it would be appropriate for it to so proceed.
- The court shall first determine whether the offender has benefited from any relevant criminal conduct; then
- The court shall make an order for the amount of such benefit; or
- The amount appearing to the court to be realisable at the time the order is made, whichever is the lower; or
- Where a victim intends or has started civil proceedings.
- The court has the power to make an order for the benefit or such lesser amount as it thinks fit.

By virtue of s74 of the Criminal Justice Act 1988, as amended by Criminal Justice Act 1993 and the Proceeds of Crime Act 1995, the amount that might be realised at the time a confiscation order is made is:

- The total of the values at that time of all the realisable property held by the defendant, less
- Where there are obligations having priority at the time the total amounts payable in pursuance of such obligations, together with the total values at that time of all gifts made or received by the defendant.

Chapter 7 – Confiscation Orders

Is there a criminal benefit?

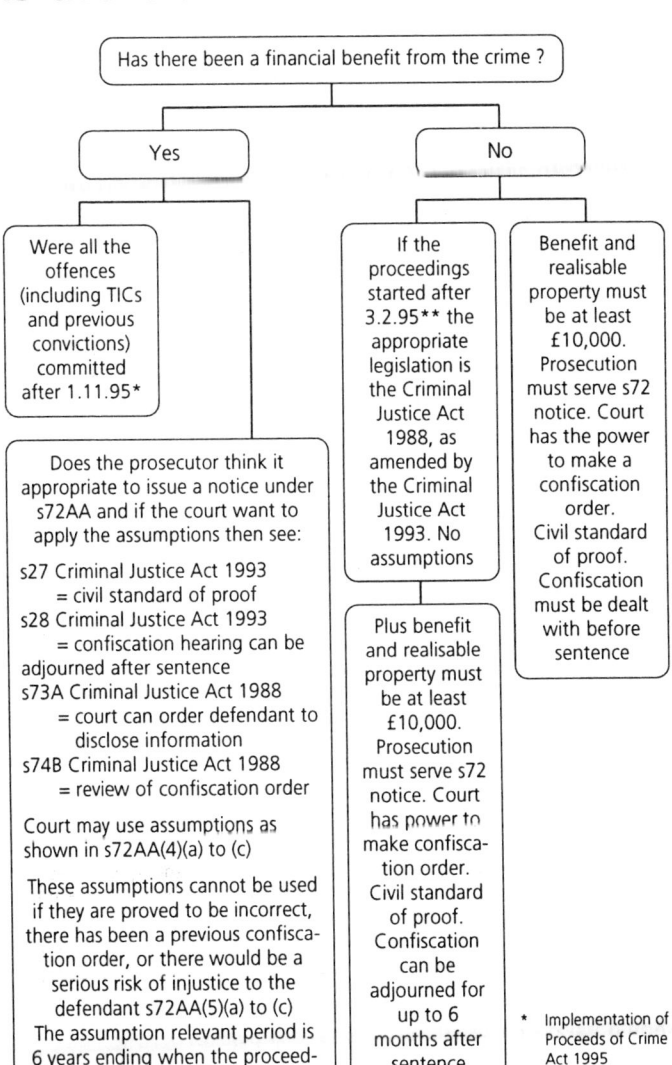

Has there been a financial benefit from the crime?

Yes

Were all the offences (including TICs and previous convictions) committed after 1.11.95*

Does the prosecutor think it appropriate to issue a notice under s72AA and if the court want to apply the assumptions then see:

s27 Criminal Justice Act 1993
= civil standard of proof
s28 Criminal Justice Act 1993
= confiscation hearing can be adjourned after sentence
s73A Criminal Justice Act 1988
= court can order defendant to disclose information
s74B Criminal Justice Act 1988
= review of confiscation order

Court may use assumptions as shown in s72AA(4)(a) to (c)

These assumptions cannot be used if they are proved to be incorrect, there has been a previous confiscation order, or there would be a serious risk of injustice to the defendant s72AA(5)(a) to (c)
The assumption relevant period is 6 years ending when the proceedings in question were instituted

No

If the proceedings started after 3.2.95** the appropriate legislation is the Criminal Justice Act 1988, as amended by the Criminal Justice Act 1993. No assumptions

Plus benefit and realisable property must be at least £10,000. Prosecution must serve s72 notice. Court has power to make confiscation order. Civil standard of proof. Confiscation can be adjourned for up to 6 months after sentence

Benefit and realisable property must be at least £10,000. Prosecution must serve s72 notice. Court has the power to make a confiscation order. Civil standard of proof. Confiscation must be dealt with before sentence

* Implementation of Proceeds of Crime Act 1995
** Statutory Instrument No 43 of 1995

113

Gift
A gift is defined as any gift made by the defendant at any time after the commission of the offence or, after the earliest of the offences to which the proceedings relate, and the court considers appropriate in all the circumstances to take the gift into account.

For the purposes of this Part of this Act circumstances in which the defendant is to be treated as making a gift include those where he transfers property to another person directly or indirectly for a consideration the value of which is significantly less than the value of the consideration provided by the defendant.

Returning to s71 of the Criminal Justice Act 1988, as amended by the Criminal Justice Act 1993 and Proceeds of Crime Act 1995, 'relevant criminal conduct' in relation to a person convicted of an offence in any proceedings before a court means that offence taken together with any other offences of a relevant description which are either:

- Offences of which he is convicted in the same proceedings; or
- Offences which the court will be taking into consideration in determining his sentence for the offence in question.

When a court makes a confiscation order against a defendant in any proceedings, it shall be its duty, in respect of any offence of which he is convicted in those proceedings, to take account of the order before:

- Imposing a fine.
- Making a compensation order.
- Making a forfeiture order.
- Making a deprivation order, but subject to that shall leave the order out of account in determining the appropriate sentence or any other manner of dealing with him.

The making of a confiscation order shall not restrict the court from dealing with an offender in any way it considers. Confiscation orders are often seen as a bargaining tool, they should never be viewed in this way and should be used to ensure that the defendant rightly loses the profits and benefit of his criminal activity.

Chapter 7 – Confiscation Orders

Section 2 Drug Trafficking Act 1994
Where a defendant appears before the Crown Court to be sentenced for a drug trafficking offence (a magistrates' court has no power to impose a drug confiscation order) it shall be the duty of the court where:

- Prosecutor gives written notice to the court that it is appropriate for court to proceed under this section; or
- Court considers, without such notice, it is appropriate for it to so proceed; then
- The Crown Court shall determine whether the offender has benefited (civil standard of proof applies) from a drug trafficking offence (see s1 of the Drug Trafficking Act 1994); then
- The court shall make an order for the amount of such benefit; or
- The amount the court determines by s5 that might be realised, whichever is the lower; or
- A nominal amount if the amount which may be realised is nil.

Section 6 Drug Trafficking Act 1994 'Amount that may be realised'
Once the value of the defendant's proceeds of drug trafficking have been established the Crown Court will decide the amount to be realised to satisfy the confiscation order.

Realisable property means:

- Any property held by the defendant; and
- Any property held by a person to whom the defendant has directly or indirectly made a gift caught by this Act (see s8).

The total amount that might be realised is the total value of the defendant's property including gifts, less the total amounts of any prior obligations or court orders.

Property is not realisable property if there is in force in respect of it an order under any of the following enactments:

- Forfeiture order under s27 of the Misuse of Drugs Act 1971.

- Deprivation order under s43 of the Powers of Criminal Courts Act 1973.
- Forfeiture order under s223 or 436 of the Criminal Procedure (Scotland) Act 1975.
- Forfeiture order under s13(2), (3) or (4) of the Prevention of Terrorism (Temporary Provisions) Act 1989.

Section 8 Drug Trafficking Act 1994 'A gift under the Act'

A gift includes the transfer of property to another for significantly less than the value of such property. A gift includes a gift made before the commencement of this Act if it was made at any time 6 years prior to proceedings being instituted, or it was made by the defendant in connection with drug trafficking carried on by him or any person or which directly or indirectly represents property received in that connection.

Where a court makes a drug trafficking confiscation order against a defendant in any proceedings, it shall be its duty, in respect of any offence of which he is convicted in those proceedings, to take account of the order before:

- Imposing a fine.
- Making any order for payment by him.
- Making a forfeiture order.
- Making a deprivation order, but subject to that shall leave the order out of account in determining the appropriate sentence or any other manner of dealing with him. The making of a confiscation order shall not restrict the court from dealing with an offender in any way it considers in respect of the offence(s).

Enforcement of Drug Trafficking Confiscation Orders

Under s32(1)(a) of the Powers of Criminal Courts Act 1973 when a Crown Court makes a confiscation order it will specify by order the magistrates' court responsible for the order's enforcement, normally the committing court.

Postponement of Determination

The courts could require further information from a defendant who makes explanation about the contents of the prosecutor's statement or volunteers his own statement or where the defendant wished more time to prepare such a statement. The following sections allow a court to postpone a case in order that the prosecutor, defendant, or the court itself has more time to adduce more information.

Section 72A Criminal Justice Act 1988
Where a court is considering making a confiscation order, it may require more information before:

- Determining whether the defendant has benefited; or
- In cases prior to the 1st November 1995 determining if benefit is £10,000 or over; or
- Determining what amount is realisable.

In order to obtain such information the court may postpone for a specified period.

Unless there are exceptional circumstances the maximum period of postponement is 6 months beginning with the date of conviction, or in an appeal against conviction the postponement shall not exceed the period ending 3 months after the date the appeal is determined or concluded.

A postponement or extension application may be made by or for the defendant, the prosecutor, or the court. Where the court exercises its power of postponement it may proceed to sentence or deal with the defendant for the offence or offences concerned.

Section 3 Drug Trafficking Act 1994
This section contains similar provisions for postponement powers for person(s) charged with drug trafficking offence(s) on or after 3rd February 1995.

Where the Crown Court is considering making a confiscation order but it considers it requires further information before:

- Determining whether the defendant has benefited from drug trafficking; or
- Determining the amount to be confiscated.

the court may postpone making a determination in order to

obtain such information. Unless there are exceptional circumstances the maximum period of postponement is 6 months beginning with the date of conviction, or in an appeal against conviction the postponement shall not exceed the period ending 3 months after the date the appeal is determined or concluded. More than one postponement may be made in the same case.

A postponement application may be made by or for the defendant, the prosecutor, or the court. Where the court exercises its power of postponement it may proceed to sentence or deal with the defendant for the offence or offences concerned.

Assumptions

Section 4 of the Drug Trafficking Act 1994 and s72AA of the Criminal Justice Act 1988, as amended, both contain legislation relating to the use of assumptions to determine whether the defendant has benefited from relevant criminal conduct, and if he has, of assessing the value of the defendant's benefit from such conduct.

The effect of the assumptions is to remove from the prosecutor the problem of proving any direct link between the defendant's property and drug trafficking or crime. The prosecutor merely needs to show that the defendant has held such property in some way or incurred an expenditure and then the burden of proof shifts to the defendant to show that the property did not come from drug trafficking or crime. The assumptions by the prosecutor and any defence put forward by the defendant are made under the civil burden of proof, being, 'the balance of probabilities'.

The difference between the assumptions in drug trafficking and crime is mainly that the court *must* make the assumption in drug cases but *may* make the assumption in crime cases. Another difference is that assumptions in drug cases cannot be made in money laundering offences under ss49, 50 and 51. However, there is no such section in the Proceeds of Crime Act 1995 amendments and therefore assumptions can be made in respect of offences under ss93A, 93B and 93C of the Criminal Justice Act 1988.

The Acts both contain sections preventing the use of the value of the defendant's proceeds of drug trafficking or crime which are the subject of a previous confiscation order. This must

Chapter 7 – Confiscation Orders

therefore apply to the making of assumptions about crime or drug proceeds and particular care should be taken not to make assumptions about property that has previously been taken into account in earlier court orders. In addition, no assumptions should be made about income or expenditure when the person concerned is serving a prison sentence or is otherwise incapacitated in a hospital or institution. However, there may be evidence to show that the incapacitation did not affect the person's criminal activities.

Section 72AA Criminal Justice Act 1988 as amended by Proceeds of Crime Act 1995

Where the defendant is convicted of a qualifying offence, in relation to proceedings before the Crown Court or a magistrates' court, to which all the following conditions are satisfied:

- It is an offence which is indictable or specified in Schedule IV.
- It is an offence which was committed after the 1st November 1995.
- The court is satisfied it is an offence from which the defendant has benefited.
- The prosecutor gives written notice.
- That notice contains a declaration that it is the prosecutor's opinion that the case is one in which assumption provisions should be applied.
- The offender:
  - is convicted in those proceedings of at least two qualifying offences (including the offence in question)
  - has been convicted of a qualifying offence on at least one previous occasion during the previous 6 years.

The court may assume:

- That any property appearing to the court:
  - to be held by the defendant at the date of conviction or at any time in the period between that date and the determination in question, or
  - to have been transferred to him at any time since the beginning of the relevant period, was received by him, at the earliest time when he appears to the court to have

held it, as a result of or in connection with the commission of offences to which Part of this Act applies; and

- That any expenditure of his since the beginning of the period of 6 years ending when the proceedings in question were instituted was met out of payments received by him as a result of or in connection with the commission of offences to which this Part of this Act applies; and
- That, for the purpose of valuing any benefit which he had or which he is assumed to have had at any time, he received the benefit free of any other interests in it.

The court shall not make such assumptions if:

- That assumption, so far as it relates to that property or expenditure, is shown to be incorrect in the defendant's case; or
- Is shown to be correct in relation to an offence the defendant's benefit from which has been the subject of a previous confiscation order; or
- That there would be (for any reason) a serious risk of injustice in the defendant's case if the assumption were to be made in relation to that property or expenditure.

Section 4 Drug Trafficking Act 1994
The Crown Court shall, for the purpose:

- Of determining whether the defendant has benefited from drug trafficking; and
- If he has, of assessing the value of his proceeds of drug trafficking, will make assumptions unless the only drug trafficking offence in respect of the defendant appearing to be sentenced is under s49, 50 or 51 of the Drug Trafficking Act 1994.

Note: The assumptions cannot be made in respect of cases arising under the 'money laundering' offences set out in this Act namely; s49 concealing or transferring the proceeds of drug trafficking, s50 assisting another person to retain the benefit of drug trafficking, and s51 acquisition, possession or use of proceeds of drug trafficking.

Chapter 7 – Confiscation Orders

The Crown Court must make the following assumptions:

- That any property appearing to the court:
  - to have been held by the defendant at anytime since his conviction; or
  - to have been transferred to him at any time since the beginning of the period of 6 years ending when the proceedings were instituted against him; was received as a payment or reward in connection with drug trafficking.
- That any expenditure of his since the beginning of that period was met out of payments received by him in connection with drug trafficking carried on by him; and
- That, for the purpose of valuing any property received or assumed to have been received by him at any time as such a reward, he received the property free of any other interests in it.

The court shall not make such assumptions if:

- That assumption is shown to be incorrect in the defendant's case; or
- Is shown to be correct in relation to an offence the defendant's benefit from which has been the subject of a previous confiscation order; or
- The court is satisfied that there would be a serious risk of injustice in the defendant's case if the assumptions were to be made.

Where, by virtue of this subsection, the court does not make one or more of the required assumptions, it shall state its reasons.

Prosecutor's Statement – Section 73 Criminal Justice Act 1988 as amended by Criminal Justice Act 1993 and Proceeds of Crime Act 1995

Where the prosecutor has given written notice to the court for the purposes of a confiscation order, or the court is proceeding of its on volition and requires a statement under this section from the prosecutor, the prosecutor shall, within such period as the court may direct, tender to the court a statement as to any relevant matters:

The Financial Investigator's Companion

- To determining whether the defendant has benefited from any relevant criminal conduct; or
- To an assessment of the value of the defendant's benefit from that conduct; and
- Where such a statement is tendered in a case in which a declaration has been made with regard to assumptions then all matters relevant to such assumptions.

Such a statement is referred to as a 'prosecutor's statement'. The prosecutor may at any time, or the court may at any time, require the prosecutor to tender to the court a further statement, within such a period as the court directs.

The prosecutor will submit a further prosecutor's statement in all case involving application under ss74A, 74B and 74C (review and revision of confiscation orders).

Where any statement has been tendered to any court by the prosecutor under this section, and the defendant accepts to any extent any allegation in the statement, the court may, for the purpose of determining whether the defendant has benefited from any relevant criminal conduct or of assessing the value of the defendant's benefit from such conduct, treat his acceptance as conclusive of the matters to which it relates.

Where the prosecutor's statement is tendered under this section, and the court is satisfied a copy has been served on the defendant, the court may require the defendant to indicate to what extent he accepts each allegation in the statement. Where he does not accept any allegation, he must indicate to the court any matters he proposes to rely on in answer to the statement.

If the defendant fails in any respect to comply with the requirement above he may be treated for the purposes of this section as accepting every allegation in the statement apart from:

- Any allegation in respect of which he has complied; and
- Any allegation that he has benefited from any offence or that any property was obtained by him as a result of or in connection with the commission of an offence.

Where the prosecutor accepts, to any extent, any information in the defendant's statement to the court as to any matters relevant in determining the amount that might be realised at the

Chapter 7 – Confiscation Orders

time the confiscation order is made, the court may, for the purpose of that determination, treat the acceptance by the prosecutor as conclusive to the matters to which it relates.

An allegation may be accepted or a matter indicated for the purposes of this section either:

- Orally before the court; or
- In writing in accordance with court rules.

Section 73A Criminal Justice Act 1988 as amended by Criminal Justice Act 1993 and Proceeds of Crime Act 1995

Where a person has been convicted of an offence of a relevant description and the prosecutor has given written notice to the court or the court is proceeding of its own volition, the court may at any time (in order to obtain information to carry out its functions under the Act) order the defendant to give it such information as may be specified in the order, in such a manner, and before such date, as may be specified in the order.

If the defendant fails, without reasonable excuse, to comply with any order under this section, the court may draw such inference from that failure as it considers appropriate.

Prosecutor's Statement – Section 11 Drug Trafficking Act 1994

Where the prosecutor has given written notice to the court for the purposes of a confiscation order, or the court is proceeding of its on volition and requires a statement under this section from the prosecutor, the prosecutor shall, within such period as the court may direct, tender to the court a statement as to any relevant matters:

- To determine whether the defendant has benefited from drug trafficking; or
- Assessing the value of his proceeds of drug trafficking.

Such a statement is referred to as a 'prosecutor's statement'. (Note: The 'prosecutor's statement' completed by a financial investigator should not contain the MG11 statutory declaration.)

The prosecutor may at any time give the court a further statement, or the court may at any time require the prosecutor to give a further statement, within such period as it may direct.

The prosecutor will provide a further statement in all cases under ss13, 14 and 15 of the Drug Trafficking Act 1994 concerning the revision of confiscation orders.

Where any prosecutor's statement has been served on the court, and a copy of the statement has been served on the defendant, it may require the defendant:

- To indicate to it, within such period as it may direct, the extent to which he accepts each allegation in the statement; and
- So far as he does not accept any such allegation, to give particulars of any matters on which he proposes to rely.

Where the defendant accepts to any extent any allegation in any prosecutor's statement, the court may treat acceptance as conclusive of the matters to which it relates, in relation to determining whether he has benefited or in assessing the value of his proceeds from drug trafficking

If the defendant fails in any respect to comply with a requirement to indicate acceptance with items in the prosecutor's statement he may be treated as accepting every allegation in the prosecutor's statement with which he has not complied.

No acceptance by the defendant under this section that any payment or other reward was received by him in connection with any drug trafficking carried on by him or another person shall be admissible in evidence in any proceedings for an offence.

When the defendant gives the Crown Court a statement as to any matters relevant to determining the amount that might be realised at the time the confiscation order is made, and the prosecutor accepts to any extent any allegation in the statement, the court may, for the purposes of that determination, treat the acceptance by the prosecutor as conclusive of the matters to which it relates. The acceptance may be in any form the court prescribes or directs.

Chapter 7 – Confiscation Orders

Review and Revision of Confiscation Orders
Criminal Justice Act 1988 as amended by Criminal Justice Act 1993 and Proceeds of Crime Act 1995

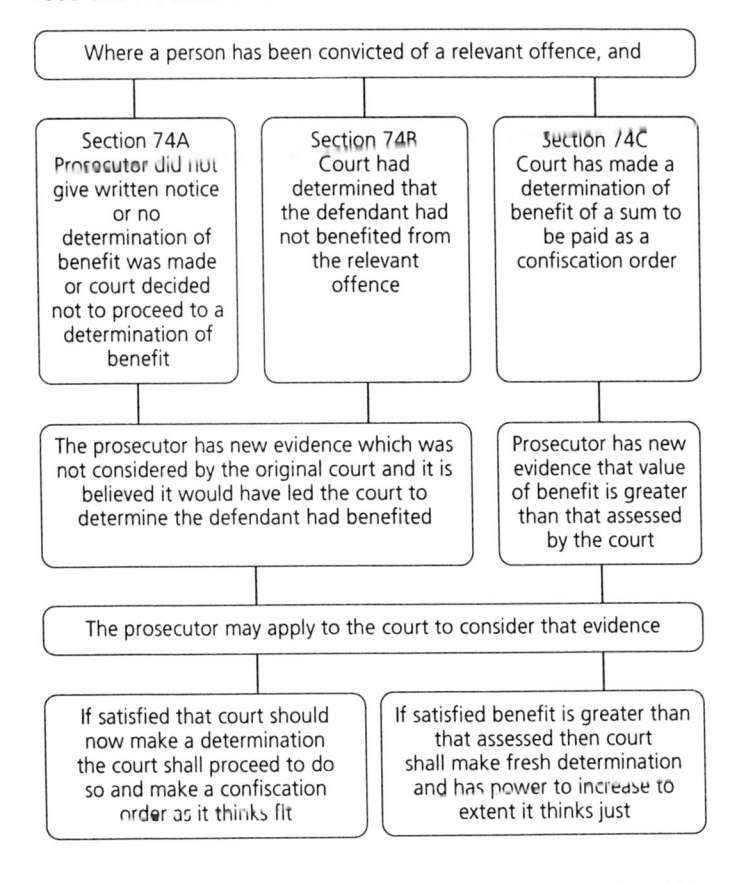

```
┌─────────────────────────────────────────────────────────────────┐
│  Where a person has been convicted of a relevant offence, and   │
└─────────────────────────────────────────────────────────────────┘
          │                    │                       │
┌───────────────────┐ ┌──────────────────┐ ┌────────────────────┐
│   Section 74A     │ │   Section 74B    │ │    Section 74C     │
│  Prosecutor did   │ │   Court had      │ │  Court has made a  │
│  not give written │ │   determined     │ │  determination of  │
│  notice or no     │ │   that the       │ │  benefit of a sum  │
│  determination of │ │   defendant had  │ │  to be paid as a   │
│  benefit was made │ │   not benefited  │ │  confiscation      │
│  or court decided │ │   from the       │ │  order             │
│  not to proceed   │ │   relevant       │ │                    │
│  to a             │ │   offence        │ │                    │
│  determination of │ │                  │ │                    │
│  benefit          │ │                  │ │                    │
└───────────────────┘ └──────────────────┘ └────────────────────┘
          │                                          │
┌──────────────────────────────────────────┐ ┌────────────────────┐
│ The prosecutor has new evidence which    │ │ Prosecutor has new │
│ was not considered by the original court │ │ evidence that      │
│ and it is believed it would have led     │ │ value of benefit   │
│ the court to determine the defendant     │ │ is greater than    │
│ had benefited                            │ │ that assessed      │
│                                          │ │ by the court       │
└──────────────────────────────────────────┘ └────────────────────┘
          │                                          │
┌─────────────────────────────────────────────────────────────────┐
│    The prosecutor may apply to the court to consider that       │
│                            evidence                             │
└─────────────────────────────────────────────────────────────────┘
          │                                          │
┌──────────────────────────────┐ ┌──────────────────────────────┐
│ If satisfied that court      │ │ If satisfied benefit is      │
│ should now make a            │ │ greater than that assessed   │
│ determination the court      │ │ then court shall make fresh  │
│ shall proceed to do so and   │ │ determination and has power  │
│ make a confiscation order    │ │ to increase to extent it     │
│ as it thinks fit             │ │ thinks just                  │
└──────────────────────────────┘ └──────────────────────────────┘
```

No application shall be entertained by the court under s74A, 74B or 74C if it is made after the end of the period of 6 years beginning with the date of conviction.

Assumptions specified in s72AA shall not be made in relation to any property unless it is property held or transferred to the defendant before the time when he was sentenced or otherwise dealt with in the case in question.

Review and Revision of Proceeds under Drug Trafficking Act 1994

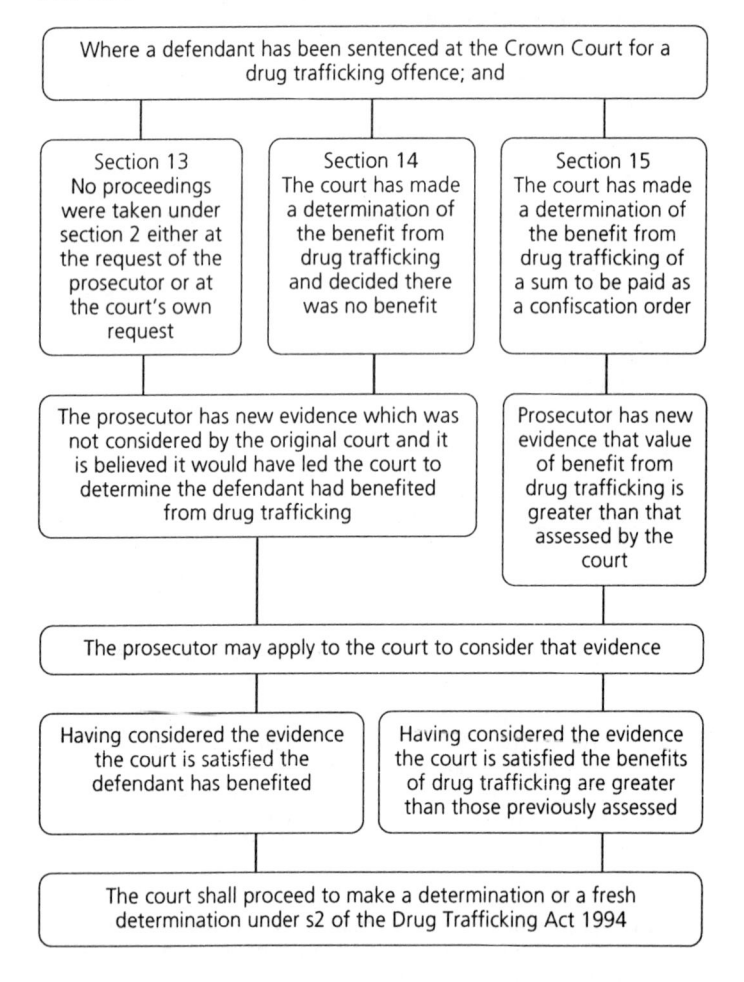

```
┌─────────────────────────────────────────────────────────────┐
│ Where a defendant has been sentenced at the Crown Court for │
│              a drug trafficking offence; and                │
└─────────────────────────────────────────────────────────────┘
```

Section 13
No proceedings were taken under section 2 either at the request of the prosecutor or at the court's own request

Section 14
The court has made a determination of the benefit from drug trafficking and decided there was no benefit

Section 15
The court has made a determination of the benefit from drug trafficking of a sum to be paid as a confiscation order

The prosecutor has new evidence which was not considered by the original court and it is believed it would have led the court to determine the defendant had benefited from drug trafficking

Prosecutor has new evidence that value of benefit from drug trafficking is greater than that assessed by the court

The prosecutor may apply to the court to consider that evidence

Having considered the evidence the court is satisfied the defendant has benefited

Having considered the evidence the court is satisfied the benefits of drug trafficking are greater than those previously assessed

The court shall proceed to make a determination or a fresh determination under s2 of the Drug Trafficking Act 1994

No application under s13, 14 or 15 shall be entertained by the court after the end of the period of 6 years beginning with the date of the last conviction.

Chapter 7 – Confiscation Orders

The court may take into account payments or rewards received after conviction if it is proved it was received in connection with drug trafficking by any person prior to that date. No assumptions under s4 can be made in respect of such rewards or where the court substitutes or makes a fresh determination it may substitute or impose a new period of imprisonment as fixed by s31(2) of the Powers of Criminal Courts Act 1973.

Chapter 8
Forfeiture Orders

Chapter 8
Forfeiture Orders

The legislation surrounding forfeiture is contained in a number of Acts all of which were in existence before the Criminal Justice Act 1988 and the Drug Trafficking Act 1994. In this chapter we will examine firstly the areas surrounding the forfeiture of property concerned in crime and drugs, and then look at the forfeiture of drugs monies forfeited as a result of their import or export and finally legislation surrounding terrorist forfeiture.

Section 43 Powers of Criminal Courts Act 1973

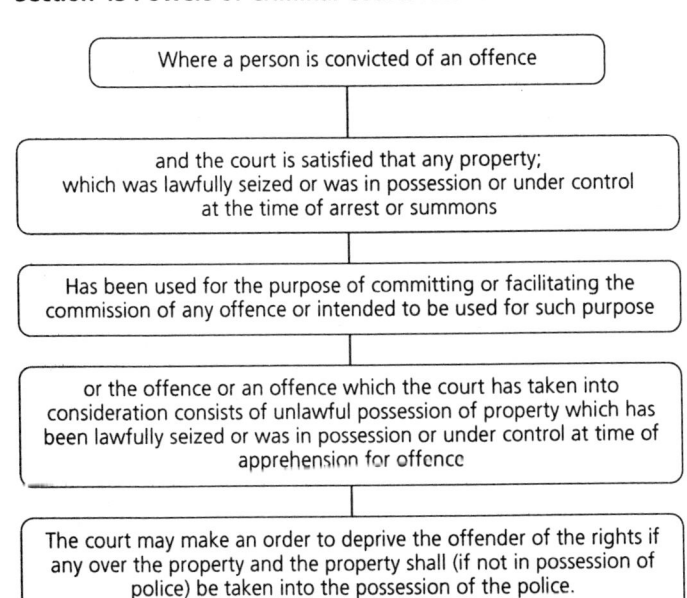

Where a person is convicted of an offence

and the court is satisfied that any property; which was lawfully seized or was in possession or under control at the time of arrest or summons

Has been used for the purpose of committing or facilitating the commission of any offence or intended to be used for such purpose

or the offence or an offence which the court has taken into consideration consists of unlawful possession of property which has been lawfully seized or was in possession or under control at time of apprehension for offence

The court may make an order to deprive the offender of the rights if any over the property and the property shall (if not in possession of police) be taken into the possession of the police.

In considering whether such order should be made the court shall have regard to the value of the property and the financial effects on the offender of the order

Section 43 was amended by s69 of the Criminal Justice Act 1988 to cover specific road traffic offences including driving, attempting to drive, or being in charge of a vehicle, in the commission of an offence under the Road Traffic Act 1988 punishable with imprisonment, or the offence of manslaughter, or wanton and furious driving under section 35 of the Offences Against the Person Act 1861.

When an order is made in respect of property which could be the subject of ownership by a third party, that third party has to make a claim under the Police Property Act 1897 within 6 months of the order. The only grounds for application are that the claimant had not consented to the offender's possession of the property, or did not know or have reason to suspect, that the property was to be used for the purpose that it was.

Section 107 of the Criminal Justice Act 1988 added s43A to s43 of the Powers of Criminal Courts Act 1973, this allowed a court making an order to specify a sum payable from the proceeds of such property to be paid to the victim of personal injury, loss or damage. This type of order should never be used to replace a compensation order if the offender appears to have other means, even though it may be to the advantage of the victim.

There have been numerous cases successfully appealed where the making of an order under s43 has been viewed as 'overdoing the punishment for the offence'. In one particular case *R v Ottey* (1984) the defendant was given the same term of imprisonment as co-defendants but was ordered to forfeit a vehicle as well. This was held to be a wrongly imposed additional penalty on Ottey whose responsibility in the crime was the same as the other defendants.

Where an order is made under s43, depriving an offender of his rights in property used to commit a crime, the primary sentence should be discounted, but this should not be done where a confiscation order is made under s71 of the Criminal Justice Act 1988 (*R v Priestly* (1995)).

The forfeiture of property in criminal cases should always be considered prior to the confiscation route and should always be applied in simple cases where the monetary value is in keeping with the crime committed. It is important to remember that the decision as to whether an application for forfeiture or

Chapter 8 – Forfeiture Orders

confiscation is to be made rests with the prosecuting authority. If confiscation is to be applied for the court will not usually be able to also make a forfeiture order (*R v Stuart & Bonner* (1989)).

Section 27 Misuse of Drugs Act 1971

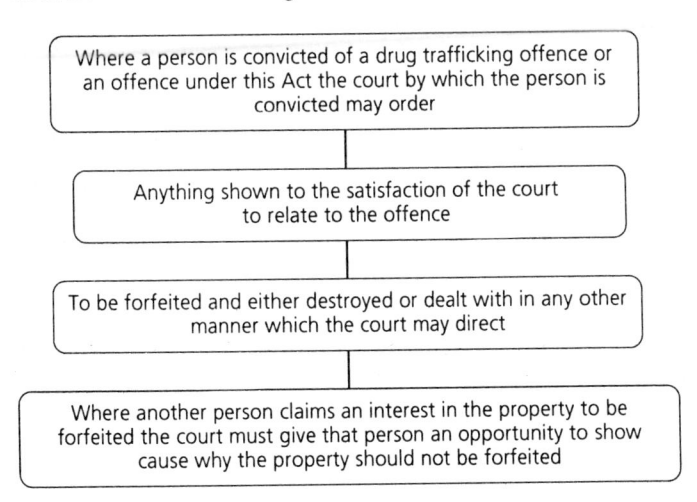

> Where a person is convicted of a drug trafficking offence or an offence under this Act the court by which the person is convicted may order

> Anything shown to the satisfaction of the court to relate to the offence

> To be forfeited and either destroyed or dealt with in any other manner which the court may direct

> Where another person claims an interest in the property to be forfeited the court must give that person an opportunity to show cause why the property should not be forfeited

The important facts to cover in any forfeiture application is that the item must be tangible and directly connected with the offence, such as apparatus for making drugs, vehicles used for conveying drugs, cash handed over or about to be exchanged for drugs or monies in the possession of a drug trafficker which form future working capital. The offender must be given the opportunity to put the facts before the court to establish that the requirements of this section are met before any decision is made on the forfeiture.

Forfeiture can never be used to assign charges on property (*R v Khan* (1982) and *R v Pearce* (1996)) or bank accounts (*R v Cuthbertson* (1981)) as it was never designed by Parliament to strip the drug trafficker of their personal assets or the profits of their enterprise but merely as a vehicle to destroy or apply the vast array of items used within the illicit drug trade. This legislation can rightly be used in cases when the sum of money in a person's possession directly relates to the offence charged, but must never be used to try and take property that is not directly relating to the offence(s) charged and convicted. The Drug Trafficking Offences Act 1986 also created a further problem in that a confiscation hearing applied in every case and only when there was no confiscation order could a forfeiture order be considered. The Drug Trafficking Act 1994 has changed this and now, providing either the court or prosecutor proceed to a confiscation hearing, then the forfeiture order may be a viable alternative. The forfeiture order deprives a defendant of the property there and then whereas a confiscation order is an order to the person to pay a sum of money in due course. Obtaining rights over the property immediately allows the property to be rapidly and efficiently disposed of or otherwise put to good use, it also allows the court to specify the manner in which they are to be dealt with.

It may be of importance to be aware of *R v Pearce* (1996) which decided that a house cannot be forfeited under s27 of the Misuse of Drugs Act 1971. It was successfully argued that 'anything' did not include real property, and therefore a house was exempt.

Chapter 8 – Forfeiture Orders

Section 42 Drug Trafficking Act 1994

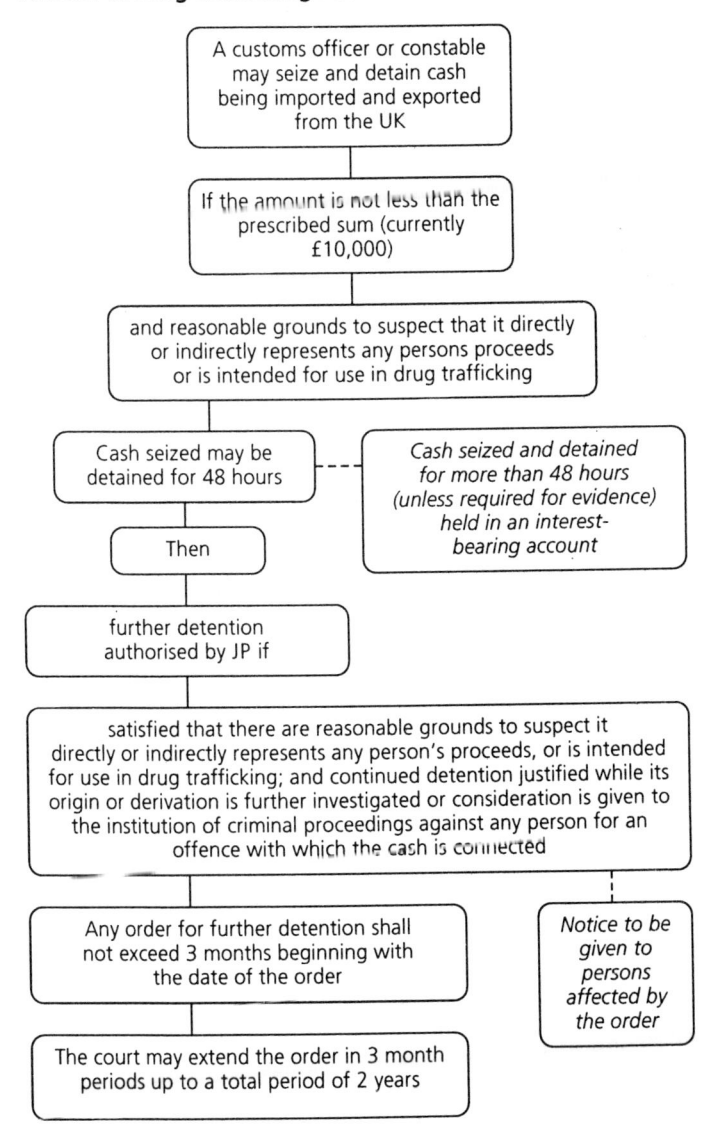

A customs officer or constable may seize and detain cash being imported and exported from the UK

↓

If the amount is not less than the prescribed sum (currently £10,000)

↓

and reasonable grounds to suspect that it directly or indirectly represents any persons proceeds or is intended for use in drug trafficking

↓

Cash seized may be detained for 48 hours — — — *Cash seized and detained for more than 48 hours (unless required for evidence) held in an interest-bearing account*

↓

Then

↓

further detention authorised by JP if

↓

satisfied that there are reasonable grounds to suspect it directly or indirectly represents any person's proceeds, or is intended for use in drug trafficking; and continued detention justified while its origin or derivation is further investigated or consideration is given to the institution of criminal proceedings against any person for an offence with which the cash is connected

↓

Any order for further detention shall not exceed 3 months beginning with the date of the order · · · *Notice to be given to persons affected by the order*

↓

The court may extend the order in 3 month periods up to a total period of 2 years

The cash detained under an order may be released on application to the magistrates' court by the person who was importing or exporting the cash, or the person on whose behalf it was being so imported or exported or any other person.

A customs officer or constable who becomes satisfied that its detention is no longer justified shall first notify the magistrates' court under whose order it is being detained.

Section 43 – A magistrates' court may order forfeiture of any cash seized under s42 if satisfied, on an application made while the cash is detained under that section, that the cash directly or indirectly represents any person's proceeds of drug trafficking, or is intended by any person for use in drug trafficking.

The standard of proof in proceedings under this section shall be those applicable to civil proceedings.

Section 45-47 refer to appeals under the above sections.

Section 13 Prevention of Terrorism (Temporary Provisions) Act 1989

The powers of forfeiture under the Prevention of Terrorism (Temporary Provisions) Act 1989 are contained under s13. Forfeiture under this legislation is directly linked to 'restraint' and therefore if any property is deemed to possibly be forfeitable advice from the Central Confiscation Bureau of the Crown Prosecution Service is recommended at the earliest opportunity.

Chapter 9
The International Perspective

Chapter 9
The International Perspective

The evolution of global initiatives to combat the international trade in drugs, crime and laundered money is protracted and complicated. Books have been written explaining how this international resolve has evolved. We have been greatly assisted by both William C Gilmore's, *Dirty Money*, published by the Council of Europe and the *International Guide to Money Laundering Law and Practice*, edited by Richard Parlour and published by Butterworths. As our book is a practitioners' guide to the investigation of money laundering and both the above books concisely document the historical evolution of global money laundering legal and social initiatives, we only propose to briefly summarise key landmarks.

There were some anti-drug initiatives early in the twentieth century, such as the International Opium Convention of 1912 and the 1931 Convention for Limiting the Manufacture and Regulating the Distribution of Narcotic Drugs. It was, however, at the end of World War II and the conception of the United Nations (UN) in 1945, that the global community started to focus their attention on the growing problems associated with the expanding illicit drug trade.

Member States of the European Economic Community, (EEC), founded in 1957 and continually expanding, have particularly since the late 1980's sought to promote enhanced co-operation in criminal matters.[1]

The Strasbourg based Council of Europe (CE) was established in 1949 to, 'promote European unity, foster social and economic progress and protect human rights'. Since the demise of the 'cold war' in the mid-1980's it has enjoyed a membership expansion with many central and eastern European countries joining. Among its many achievements are the 1957 European Convention on Extradition, and the 1959 European Convention on Mutual Assistance in Criminal Matters.

---

[1] *The UK applied to join the European Economic Community in 1963 but was prevented from doing so by a French veto. The UK eventually joined in 1973.*

The 1988 UN 'Convention against illicit traffic in narcotic drugs and psychotropic substances (extracts)' succeeded in emphasising internationally the serious problem of the illicit drug trade. The Convention agreed on a number of Articles, all of which the parties accepted, and agreed to introduce into their domestic laws. The agreement covered legal definitions, scope of agreement, offences and sanctions, jurisdiction, confiscation, extradition, mutual legal assistance, transfer of proceedings and other forms of co-operation and training.

In July 1989 in Paris at the Summit Meeting of the Heads of State or Government of the 7 major industrial nations, commonly known as the Group of Seven, it was decided that there was an urgent need for action against illicit drug production, consumption, trafficking and money laundering, both nationally and internationally. As a result, the Financial Action Task Force (FATF) was created and it is this organisation that has had a profound influence on counter-measures within the global community. In 1990 the FATF made a number of recommendations which emphasised the 1988 UN Convention Articles. The FATF has and is practically assisting national organisations and governments to achieve the goals set out in those Articles and Recommendations. The positive practical impact of the FATF in combating the global disease associated with illicit drugs cannot be emphasised enough. It is important that the financial investigator is acquainted with reports disseminated by the FATF as it is dedicated to discovering new money laundering techniques.

In 1990 the CE held a 'Convention on laundering, search, seizure and confiscation of the proceeds of crime', and agreed on 44 Articles similar to the 1988 UN Convention Articles.

On the 10th June 1994 the EEC issued a Council Directive, 'on prevention of the use of the financial system for the purpose of money laundering' (91/308/EEC) which referred to the 1988 UN Convention, 1990 CE Convention and to the declaration of principles adopted in December 1988 in Basle by the banking supervisory authorities of the Group of Ten.

All of the international efforts to combat the illicit drug trade, crime and money laundering will fail if the resolve of individual nations waivers. In the UK, Parliament has responded to the international conventions by passing domestic legislation

Chapter 9 – The International Perspective

and creating the Home Office Central Authority to deal with mutual assistance requests to and from nations around the world. The International Criminal Police Organisation (Interpol) (ICPO) assists in communication between police investigators throughout the world. In the UK, ICPO and the National Criminal Intelligence Service (NCIS) who acts as a catalyst and disseminator of intelligence, work closely together.

So let us examine how an active financial investigator working in England and Wales is affected and assisted by the above international agreements. In the UK, the Criminal Justice (International Co-operation) Act 1990 and the above Conventions on Mutual Assistance in Criminal Matters are the principal sources of mutual assistance powers and the Central Authority is responsible for dealing with requests to and from the UK. As multilateral and bilateral treaties and agreements are constantly being made it is therefore important for the investigator to liaise with the Central Authority as soon as possible in order to follow the current correct method of international communication. Its address is as follows:

The United Kingdom Central Authority
(for Mutual Legal Assistance in Criminal Matters),
C7 Division,
Home Office,
50 Queen Anne's Gate,
London SW1H 9AT.

The Central Authority has produced an extremely informative guideline booklet entitled 'International Mutual Legal Assistance in Criminal Matters', published by HMSO, and which all financial investigators should possess. Current methods of communicating with the Central Authority are contained in the latest reprint.

Police-to-police requests for mutual assistance, particularly with regard to information or intelligence during preliminary stages of an investigation, can be sent or received through ICPO and do not need a formal Letter of Request. In some countries a Letter of Request is known as a Commission Rogatoire.

Formal requests between countries of differing judicial systems are made through diplomatic channels on Letters of Request. In the UK, the Central Authority acts as a conduit through which request are forwarded to other jurisdictions from the UK and requests from other jurisdictions are received and actioned. Letters of Request would be needed for the following matters: the service of process; to obtain written evidence both at the investigation or prosecution stages; to enable persons in detention to appear as witnesses, or otherwise assist proceedings; to permit search and seizure and make provision for the certification of evidence where necessary. Authorised UK sources for issuing Letters of Request are its designated Law Officers and public prosecutors namely: the Attorney General for England and Wales; the Director of Public Prosecutions; Crown Prosecutors; the Serious Fraud Office; the Investigations Division of the Department of Trade and Industry; any Assistant Secretary (Legal) in charge of a Prosecution Division of HM Customs and Excise; the Lord Advocate; Procurators Fiscal; the Director of Public Prosecutions for Northern Ireland; and the Attorney General for Northern Ireland.

Basically the Letter of Request is a formal communication between the designated law offices in one country and the designated law offices in another country. In the UK, the Central Authority facilitates this communication through diplomatic channels. In urgent cases ICPO can assist in this communication process. In some urgent cases the Central Authority can contact the foreign designated law office direct. The Letter of Request will show the designated authority making the request, it will detail the purpose of the request, summarise the case and clearly describe the offences showing what law they violate, it will show any relevant dates, ie trial or other reasons for urgency, and it may ask for the investigating officer to be present. Officers travelling abroad must be diplomatic and sensitive to laws, practices and customs in other jurisdictions. Officers must restrict their inquires to those contained in the Letter of Request and authorised by the relevant designated authority. A well-drafted Letter of Request will also contain a paragraph to allow, 'further consequential inquires as appear appropriate from the making of inquiries outlined above'. In many foreign jurisdictions an Examining Magistrate will authorise, and in some cases carry out, inquiries in the Letter of Request — the visiting officer will be guided by the hosts.

Evidence abroad must be obtained in accordance with the laws and procedures of the country concerned. Admissibility of

Chapter 9 – The International Perspective

evidence obtained abroad can be dealt with as follows:

- Tendered at committal – s102(2) of the Magistrates' Courts Act 1980
- Statement may be read at Crown Court with the consent of the defence – s10(1) and (2) of the Criminal Justice Act 1967
- Can only be read at Crown Court without defence permission if the maker of the statement is outside the UK and it is not reasonably practical to secure their attendance – s23 of the Criminal Justice Act 1988
- Evidence may be admitted in the interest of justice – s25 of the Criminal Justice Act 1988. Witness summonses can be arranged – s2 of the Criminal Justice (International Co-Operation) Act 1990.

Financial investigators may be requested to facilitate inquiries by visiting foreign investigators, these will be conducted under UK law.

In 1990 the Home Office set up the Central Drug Fund to assist in defraying the cost of inquiries into the assets of drug traffickers and/or their laundered money. In order to apply for expenses from the fund there are strict guidelines to follow, it is therefore advisable that the current guidelines are obtained from the Central Fund Administrator, Home Office, 50 Queen Anne's Gate, London SW1H 9AT, as soon as there is a likelihood of a trip abroad.

It will be the responsibility of the officer travelling abroad to arrange an interpreter, you may wish to take one from the UK or hire one locally. The local police or British Consulate may be able to help with the hire of local interpreters however it is always best to arrange this before leaving the UK.

When a financial investigator has been requested to carry out inquiries abroad they may also need permission from a senior officer of their organisation.

'Estimates of dirty money range from 300 to 500 thousand million US dollars available each year for money laundering. It is obvious that these huge quantities of money, often linked with organised crime, threaten the stability of financial institutions and, ultimately, democracy and the rule of law.' Not to mention the crisis in society as it struggles with the evil and heartache created by illicit drugs and associated dirty money. Financial investigators are the key in this global battle but must realise that their activities are cutting off the life blood of depraved and desperate men and women, consequently the investigator should be alert at all times.

Appendix I
Sample Production Orders & Warrants

Appendix I – Sample Production Orders & Warrants

[NAME] POLICE SERVICE

DRUG TRAFFICKING PROCEDURE

FORCE CREST

Information to Support an Application for Production Order

Section 55 Drug Trafficking Act 1994

The information of *[name of officer]*,

of *[name of force and unit to which attached]*.

Who upon oath (affirmation) states:

a) There are reasonable grounds for suspecting that *[name of suspect]* has carried on or has benefited from drug trafficking, and

b) There are reasonable grounds for suspecting that the material to which this application relates:
   i) is likely to be of substantial value (by itself or together with other material) to the investigation for the purpose of which this application is made, and
   ii) does not consist or include items subject to legal privilege or excluded material.

c) There are reasonable grounds for believing that it is in the public interest, having regard:
   i) to the benefit likely to accrue to the investigation if the material is obtained, and
   ii) to the circumstances under which the person in possession of the material holds it
   that the material should be produced or that access to it should be given.

The material to which this information applies is *[state the details of all material sought]*.

The person(s) organisation(s) holding the material and the premises to which this information applies are *[state name and address of persons or company holding the information]*.

Signature .... Date ....

Appendix I – Sample Production Orders & Warrants

[NAME] CROWN COURT

DRUG TRAFFICKING PROCEDURE

COURT CREST

Production Order

Section 55 Drug Trafficking Act 1994

To [name of person or company to whom order is addressed].

An application having been made in pursuance of Section 55 of the Drug Trafficking Act 1994 by [name of officer and police force to which attached].

That you should give a constable access to and supply such originals and copies as may be necessary of the material to which the said application relates, namely: [details of items sought as set out in the information] and any correspondence concerning any transactions in relation to the dealings with: [names and account details of persons concerned].

I am satisfied after hearing the parties to the application that the conditions in subsection (4) of Section 55 are fulfilled in relation thereto.

COURT STAMP

You are hereby ordered to:

[produce the said material to a constable for him to take away]

[give a constable access to the said material]

not later than [7 days or specify the alternative period].

Signature of Circuit Judge .... Date ....

Formal title of Circuit Judge ....

Note

Disclosing information about this order may contravene Section 58 of the Drug Trafficking Act 1994. If you are contacted by anyone concerning this order you may wish to seek legal advice, or contact [name of officer] on [telephone number of officer] before disclosure is made.

Appendix I – Sample Production Orders & Warrants

[NAME] POLICE SERVICE

DRUG TRAFFICKING PROCEDURE

FORCE CREST

Information in Support of Application for a Search Warrant

Section 56(2)(a) Drug Trafficking Act 1994

The information of *[name of officer]*,

of *[force and department details]*.

Who upon oath (affirmation) states:

That an order made on *[date production order granted]* under Section 55 of the Drug Trafficking Act 1994 in relation to material on the specified premises has not been complied with.

The material to which this information applies is *[details of material sought as set out in original production order]*.

The premises to which this application applies are *[name and address of institution or person in possession of the material]*.

Signature .... Date ....

Appendix I – Sample Production Orders & Warrants

[NAME] POLICE SERVICE

DRUG TRAFFICKING PROCEDURE

FORCE CREST

Information in Support of Application for a Search Warrant
Section 56(2)(b) Drug Trafficking Act 1994

The information of *[name of officer]*,

of *[force and department details]*.

Who upon oath (affirmation) states:

a) There are reasonable grounds for suspecting that *[name of suspect]* has carried on or has benefited from drug trafficking, and

b) There are reasonable grounds for suspecting that there is material on the premises to which the application relates which:
   i) is likely to be of substantial value (by itself or with other material) to the investigation for the purpose of which the application is made, and
   ii) does not consist of, or include items subject to legal privilege or excluded material, and

c) There are reasonable grounds for believing that it is in the public interest, having regard:
   i) to the benefit likely to accrue to the investigation if the material is obtained, and
   ii) to the circumstances under which the person in possession of the material holds it, that the material should be produced or that access should be given to it, and

d) It would not be appropriate to make an order under section 55 in relation to the material because *[it is not practicable to communicate with any person entitled to produce the material] [it is not practicable to communicate with any person entitled to grant access to the material or entitled to grant entry to the premises on which the material is situated] [the investigation for the purposes of which the application is made might be seriously prejudiced unless a constable could secure immediate access to the material]*.

The material to which this information applies is *[details of material sought]*.

The premises to which this application applies are *[name and address of institution or person in possession of the material]*.

Signature .... Date ....

Appendix I – Sample Production Orders & Warrants

[NAME] POLICE SERVICE

DRUG TRAFFICKING PROCEDURE

FORCE CREST

Information in Support of Application for a Search Warrant

Section 56(2)(c) Drug Trafficking Act 1994

The information of *[name of officer]*,

of *[force and department details]*.

Who upon oath (affirmation) states:

a) There are reasonable grounds for suspecting that *[details of suspect]* has carried on or has benefited from drug trafficking, and

b) There are reasonable grounds for suspecting that there is material on the premises to which the application relates relating to the person specified at (a) above, or to the question of whether that person has benefited from drug trafficking, or to any question as to the extent or whereabouts of the proceeds of drug trafficking which is likely to be of substantial value (by itself or with other material) to the investigation for the purpose of which the application is made but the material cannot, at the moment be particularised, and

(c) That (it is not practicable to communicate with any person entitled to grant entry to the premises) (entry to the premises will not be granted unless a warrant is produced) (the investigation for the purpose of which the application is made might be seriously prejudiced unless a constable arriving at the premises could secure immediate entry to them).

The material that can be particularised at present is *[state broad species of material sought if possible]*.

The premises to which this application relates are *[name and address of institution[s] or person[s] in possession of the material]*.

Signature .... Date ....

Appendix I – Sample Production Orders & Warrants

[NAME] CROWN COURT

DRUG TRAFFICKING PROCEDURE

COURT CREST

Warrant to Enter and Search Premises

Section 56 Drug Trafficking Act 1994

To each and all of the Constables of the Metropolitan Police Force.

An application having been made on *[date]* in pursuance of Section 56 of the Drug Trafficking Act 1994 by *[name of officer]* of *[unit to which attached]*.

I am satisfied that there are reasonable grounds for believing that *[name of suspect]* has carried on or benefited from drug trafficking and there is at *[name and address of institution or person in possession of the material]*.

Material likely to be (by itself or with other material) of substantial value to the investigation, namely (material which at this time cannot be specified but which is believed to directly relate to the drug trafficking activities of the suspect) and the issue of a warrant is appropriate by reason of subsections (2)(a), (3), (4) of Section 56.

Authority is hereby given for any constable accompanied by [it is not necessary to identify persons accompanying by name, a description such as 'official receiver' or 'official valuer' will suffice] to enter on one occasion only within one month from the date of this warrant the said premises and to search them for the material in respect of which the application is made.

COURT STAMP

Signature of Circuit Judge ....

Formal title of Circuit Judge ....

Date .... Time ....

A copy of this warrant should be left with the occupier or in his absence a person who appears in charge of the premises or if no such person is present in a prominent place on the premises.

Note
Disclosure of information about this investigation may contravene Section 58 of the Drug Trafficking Act 1994. If you are contacted by anyone in connection with this warrant you may wish to seek legal advice or contact *[name of officer and contact tel. number]* before disclosure is made.

Appendix I – Sample Production Orders & Warrants

REAR PAGE OF WARRANT
(TO ENTER AND SEARCH PREMISES)

Endorsement

The officer in charge of the search is responsible for the completion of this endorsement.

1. The following items sought were found.*
   No item sought was found.*

   ....
   ....

2. The following items other than those sought were seized.*
   No other item was seized.*

   ....
   ....

3. The search was conducted on *[date]* between
   ..... am/pm* and ..... am/pm* by *[name all officers present]*.

   ....
   ....

4. A copy of this warrant was handed to the occupier/person in charge of premises * or left on the premises * *[specify where]*.

   ....
   ....

Signature .... Date ....
Name, Rank, Number ....
Station and Unit to which attached ....

* Delete as necessary

Appendix I – Sample Production Orders & Warrants

[NAME OF POLICE SERVICE OR FORCE]

CRIMINAL CONDUCT PROCEDURE

FORCE CREST

Information to Support an Application for Production Order

Section 93H Criminal Justice Act 1988

The information of *[name of officer]*,

of *[name of force and unit to which attached]*.

Who upon oath (affirmation) states:

a) There are reasonable grounds for suspecting that *[name of suspect)* may have benefited from any criminal conduct, or the whereabouts or the extent of proceeds of such criminal conduct are sought.

b) There are reasonable grounds for suspecting that the material to which this application relates:
   i) is likely to be of substantial value (by itself or together with other material) to the investigation for the purpose of which this application is made, and
   ii) does not consist of or include items subject to legal privilege or excluded material, and

c) There are reasonable grounds for believing that it is in the public interest, having regard:
   i) to the benefit likely to accrue to the investigation if the material is obtained, and
   ii) to the circumstances under which the person in possession of the material holds it that the material should be produced or that access should be given to it.

The material to which this application applies is *[state full details of material sought]* and any correspondence concerning any transactions in relation to *[full name or names used]*.

The person(s)/organisation(s) holding the material and the premises to which this application relates are *[state full name and address[es] details of person[s] or organisation[s]] holding material and address[es] on which material is believed to be held]*.

Signature .... Date ....

Name of police service ....

Appendix I – Sample Production Orders & Warrants

[NAME] CROWN COURT

CRIMINAL CONDUCT PROCEDURE

CREST

Production Order

Section 93H Criminal Justice Act 1988

To *[state person or organisation who appears to be in possession of material sought]*.

An application having been made by *[name of officer and police force attached]* in pursuance of Section 93H of the Criminal Justice Act 1988 that you should give a constable access to and supply such originals and copies as necessary of the material to which the application relates namely *[list documents as set out in the information]* and any material concerning any transactions in relation to dealings with *[names used by suspect or other concerned parties]*.

I am satisfied after hearing the parties to the application that the conditions in sub section (4) of Section 93H are fulfilled in relation thereto.

COURT STAMP

You are hereby ordered to:

[produce the said material to a constable for him to take away]

[give a constable access to the said material]

not later than *[7 days or specify the alternative period]*.

Signature of Circuit Judge .... Date ....

Formal title of Circuit Judge .... Time ....

Note
Disclosure of information about this order may contravene Section 93D of the Criminal Justice Act 1988. If you are contacted by anyone concerning this order you may wish to seek legal advice, or contact *[name of officer]* on *[telephone number of officer]* before disclosure is made.

Appendix I – Sample Production Orders & Warrants

[NAME] POLICE SERVICE

CRIMINAL CONDUCT PROCEDURE

FORCE CREST

Information to Support an Application for a Search Warrant
Section 93 I(2)(a) Criminal Justice Act 1988

The information of *[name of officer and details of force or unit to which attached]*.

Who on oath (affirmation) states:

That an order made on *[date]* under Section 93H of the Criminal Justice Act 1988 has not been complied with.

The material to which this information applies is *[complete list of material sought identical to that contained in the original production order under 93H]*.

The premises to which this application applies are *[name and address of person[s] or organisation[s] in possession of material as set out in original 93H application]*.

Signature .... Date ....

Appendix I – Sample Production Orders & Warrants

[NAME] POLICE SERVICE

CRIMINAL CONDUCT PROCEDURE

FORCE CREST

Information to Support an Application for a Search Warrant

Section 93I(2)(b) Criminal Justice Act 1988

The information of *[name of officer and details of force or unit to which attached]*.

Who on oath (affirmation) states:

a) There are reasonable grounds for suspecting that *[details of suspect]* may have benefited from any criminal conduct, or the extent or whereabouts of such benefit from criminal conduct are sought, and

b) There are reasonable grounds for suspecting that there is material on the premises to which application relates which:
   i) is likely to be of substantial value (by itself or with other material) to the investigation for the purpose of which the application is made, and,
   ii) does not consist of or include material subject to legal privilege or excluded material, and

c) There are reasonable grounds for believing that it is in the public interest, having regard:
   i) to the benefit likely to accrue to the investigation if the material is obtained, and
   ii) to the circumstances under which the person in possession of the material holds it, that the material should be produced or that access should be given to it.

(d) It would not be appropriate to make an order under section 93H in relation to the material because *(it is not practicable to communicate with any person entitled to produce the material) (it is not practicable to communicate with any person entitled to grant access to the material or entitled to grant entry to the premises on which the material is situated) (the investigation for the purposes of which the application is made might be seriously prejudiced unless a constable could secure immediate access to the material)*.

The material to which this information applies is *[details of material sought]*.

The premises to which this application applies are *[name and address of institution or person in possession of the material]*.

Signature .... Date ....

Appendix I – Sample Production Orders & Warrants

[NAME] POLICE SERVICE

CRIMINAL CONDUCT PROCEDURE

FORCE CREST

Information to Support an Application for a Search Warrant

Section 93 I(2)(c) Criminal Justice Act 1988

The information of *[name of officer and details of force or unit to which attached]*.

Who on oath (affirmation) states:

a) There are reasonable grounds for suspecting that *[details of suspect]* may have benefited from criminal conduct, or the extent or whereabouts of such benefit from criminal conduct are sought, and

b) There are reasonable grounds for suspecting that there is material on the premises to which the application relates relating to the person specified at (a) above, or to the question of whether that person has benefited from any criminal conduct, or to any question as to the extent or whereabouts of the proceeds of any criminal conduct which is likely to be of substantial value (by itself or with other material) to the investigation for the purpose of which the application is made but the material cannot, at the moment be particularised, and

c) That *(it is not practicable to communicate with any person entitled to grant entry to the premises) (entry to the premises will not be granted unless a warrant is produced) (the investigation for the purpose of which the application is made might be seriously prejudiced unless a constable arriving at the premises could secure immediate entry to them)*.

The material particulars of which are known and to which this application relates are *[details of any material which can be particularised]*.

The premises to which this application relates are *[name and address of institution or person in possession of the material]*.

Signature .... Date ....

Appendix I – Sample Production Orders & Warrants

[NAME] CROWN COURT

CRIMINAL CONDUCT PROCEDURE

COURT CREST

Warrant to Enter and Search Premises

Section 93I Criminal Justice Act 1988

To each and all of the Constables of the *[name of police force]*.

An application having been made on *[date]* in pursuance of Section 93I of the Criminal Justice Act 1988, by *[name of officer]* of *[unit to which attached]*.

I am satisfied that there are reasonable grounds for believing that:

a) An order made under Section 93H has not been complied with, or

b) There are reasonable grounds for believing that *[name of suspect]* has benefited from any criminal conduct or the extent or whereabouts of such criminal conduct are sought and there is at *[name and address of institution or person in possession of the material]*.

Material likely to be (by itself or with other material) of substantial value to the investigation, namely *[details of material or material which at this time cannot be specified but which relates to criminal conduct]*.

And the issue of a warrant is appropriate by reason of subsection ((2) (a) (b) (c)) of section 93I.

Authority is hereby given for any constable accompanied by *(it is not necessary to identify persons accompanying by name, a description such as 'official receiver' or 'official valuer' will suffice)* to enter on one occasion only within one month from the date of this warrant the said premises and to search them for the material in respect of which the application is made.

COURT STAMP

Signature of Circuit Judge ....
Formal title of Circuit Judge ....
Date .... Time ....

A copy of this warrant should be left with the occupier or in his absence a person who appears in charge of the premises or if no such person is present in a prominent place on the premises.

Note
Disclosure of information about this investigation may contravene Section 93D of the Criminal Justice Act 1988. If you are contacted by anyone in connection with this warrant you may wish to seek legal advice or contact *[name of officer and contact telephone number]* before disclosure is made.

Appendix I – Sample Production Orders & Warrants

REAR PAGE OF WARRANT
(TO ENTER AND SEARCH PREMISES)

Endorsement

_____

The officer in charge of the search is responsible for the completion of this endorsement.

1. The following items sought were found.*
   No item sought was found.*

   ....
   ....

2. The following items other than those sought were seized.*
   No other item was seized.*

   ....
   ....

3. The search was conducted on *[date]* between
   ..... am/pm* and ..... am/pm* by *[name all officers present]*.

   ....
   ....

4. A copy of this warrant was handed to the occupier/person in charge of premises * or left on the premises * *[specify where]*.

   ....
   ....

Signature ....   Date ....

Name, Rank, Number ....

Station and Unit to which attached ....

* Delete as necessary

Appendix II
Sample Prosecutor's Statements

Sample Prosecutor's Statements

There is no statutory format for a prosecutor's statement, the following are suggested formats for straightforward cases. In complicated cases, advice should be sought from the Central Confiscation Bureau who are well versed with the requirements of the Acts and the dates when amendments commenced.

Appendix II – Sample Prosecutor's Statements

Section 73 Criminal Justice Act 1988 Prosecutor's Statement

IN THE MATTER OF REGINA

-v-

[FULL NAME OF DEFENDANT]

Prosecutor's Statement

Pursuant to Section 73 Criminal Justice Act 1988

This statement is prepared by *[name of officer of whatever unit and address]*.

Enquiries have been made by me into the financial affairs of the defendant *[full name]* in order to establish:

1) The benefit derived by that person in relation to the offences to which these proceedings relate, and

2) The extent, amount, nature and value of all realisable property which may be used to satisfy any Confiscation Order made by the court.

I have restricted my enquiries to a period of 6 years prior to the defendant being charged with the offences to which these proceedings relate. The offences to which these proceedings relate can be summarised as follows:
[brief summary of case including whether cases were committed since 1st November 1995, and why they meet the criteria set out in s71(1)(d) and (e)].

The total benefit obtained by the defendant as a result of the alleged offences is calculated as follows:

Count 1 *[Include here full details of benefit obtained within the charge]*

Total Benefit Derived = £xxx

Count 2 *[Include again full details of benefit obtained within the charge]*

Total Benefit Derived = £xxx

The history of the defendant as known to me includes the following:
[set out here all details of any previous convictions, and any other past orders which may be outstanding or relevant].

Appendix II – Sample Prosecutor's Statements

In the course of my investigations I have been able to trace the following sources of legitimate income:
[only include here any confirmed income including DSS and document any references to documentary exhibits].

The defendant also claimed the following legitimate incomes:
[include here any claims by the defendant of income which you have not been able to confirm or which is not accepted by the prosecution as genuine].

These incomes are of doubtful origin because they lack any form of documentation or evidence to substantiate their origins and therefore the prosecution do not accept they came about in a lawful manner.
[Here also you should highlight the areas that do not tally such as no tax returns, VAT returns, or other business-like material to back up the defendant's assertions.]

In order to calculate the defendant's proceeds of criminal conduct I have made the following assumptions using the powers set out under s72AA(4) Criminal Justice Act 1988 as amended by the Proceeds of Crime Act 1995.

1) All property received by the defendant since 1.11.95* was free of any other interest in it and as a result of committing offences to which this Act applies.

2) All expenditure by the defendant since 1.11.95* were met out of payments from or in connection with the commission of offences to which this Act applies.

3) The prosecution are satisfied there are no grounds to believe that such assumptions are incorrect or for any reason would cause a serious risk of injustice in this case if those assumptions are made.

   * This date is the commencement of the Act and until 6 years have lapsed is the date operative for the assumptions then the operative date will be 6 years prior to the commencement of proceedings.

The benefit calculated and assumed to be the proceeds of offences committed under this Act is as follows:

Expenditure	£xxx
Property Received	£xxx
Total Assumed Benefit	**£xxx**

Appendix II – Sample Prosecutor's Statements

The defendant has the following property which might be realised as follows:

Matrimonial Home	£xxx
Motor Vehicle	£xxx
Any other Property	£xxx
Bank/Building Society A/C	£xxx
Property subject of Restraint Order	£xxx
Total Realisable Property	**£xxx**

The following property is the subject of civil proceedings:
[include here all property which is the subject of repossession proceedings, mareva injunctions, or other civil actions which may affect their value, which have been notified to Prosecution. This section should set out details of all property howsoever obtained which could realise proceeds to satisfy a confiscation order.]

If the court decides to make a confiscation order the prosecution claim the position is as follows:

Total Benefit	£xxx
Total Realisable Property	£xxx
Possible Confiscation Order	**£xxx**

The effect of a confiscation order on compensation is to allow sums which the defendant cannot pay in compensation to be recovered from realised sums paid in satisfaction of the confiscation order.

Any answer or reply to this statement under Part VI of the Criminal Justice Act 1988 should be addressed to *[name and address of Crown Court]* and a copy sent to the Central Confiscation Bureau at 50, Ludgate Hill, London EC4M 7EX.

Note any advice or assistance on completion of a Prosecutor's Statement should be obtained from the Central Confiscation Bureau.

Signature ....   Date ....

Statement tendered by *[name and address of CPS Branch or Confiscation Unit]*.

Appendix II – Sample Prosecutor's Statements

Section 11 Drug Trafficking Act 1994

IN THE MATTER OF REGINA

-v-

[FULL NAME OF DEFENDANT]

Prosecutor's Statement

Pursuant to Section 11 Drug Trafficking Act 1994

This statement is prepared by [name of officer of whatever unit and address].

Enquiries have been made by me into the financial affairs of the defendant [full name] in order to establish:

1) The benefit derived by that person in relation to drug trafficking offences to which these proceedings relate, and

2) The extent, amount, nature and value of all realisable property which may be used to satisfy any Confiscation Order made by the court.

I have restricted my enquiries to a period of 6 years prior to the defendant being charged with the offences to which these proceedings relate.

The offences to which these proceedings relate can be summarised as follows:

Count 1   [Provide here a brief summary of case including details of quantities and types of drugs found and any other relevant evidence to show a dealer's lifestyle]

The total benefit obtained by the defendant as a result of the alleged offences is calculated as follows:

Count 1   [Include here full details of benefit obtained within the charge]

Total Benefit Derived = £xxx

The history of the defendant as known to me includes the following: [set out here all details of any previous convictions, and any other past orders which may be outstanding or relevant].

Appendix II – Sample Prosecutor's Statements

In the course of my investigations I have been able to trace the following sources of legitimate income:
[only include here any confirmed income including DSS and document any references to documentary exhibits].

The defendant also claimed the following legitimate incomes:
[include here any claims by the defendant of income which you have not been able to confirm or which is not accepted by the prosecution as genuine].

These incomes are of doubtful origin because they lack any form of documentation or evidence to substantiate their origins and therefore the prosecution do not accept they came about in a lawful manner.
[Here also you should highlight the areas that do not tally such as no tax returns, VAT returns, or other business-like material to back up the defendant's assertions.]

In order to calculate the defendant's proceeds of drug trafficking I have made the following assumptions using the powers set out under the Drug Trafficking Act 1994:

1) All property received by the defendant up to 6 years prior to the charges being proffered in this case were free of any other interests in it and as a result of committing offences to which this Act applies.

2) All expenditure by the defendant up to 6 years prior to the charges being proffered were met out of payments from or in connection with the commission of offences to which this Act applies.

3) The prosecution are satisfied there are no grounds to believe that such assumptions are incorrect or for any reason would cause a serious risk of injustice in this case if those assumptions are made.

I calculate the defendant's proceeds of drug trafficking as follows:
[Include here any unexplained monies, transfers of assets by way of gifts to others, unexplained expenditures, any acquired assets, and cash seized at time of arrest. You may also need to refer to the relevant sections in Section 4 of the Act.]

The defendant has the following property which might be realised as follows:

Matrimonial Home	£xxx
Motor Vehicle	£xxx
Any other Property	£xxx
Bank/Building Society A/C	£xxx
Property subject of Restraint Order	£xxx
Total realisable property	**£xxx**

Appendix II – Sample Prosecutor's Statements

If you suspect that the defendant has secreted assets you may use the following:

The prosecution have been unable to obtain details of the defendant's foreign bank accounts or identify the assets which he is believed to hold in other unknown property, *[then include documents on which you rely to make this suggestion]* the Act allows the court to ask questions of the defendant in respect of these matters and it is suggested this course of action is taken.

If you have obtained any restraint orders prior to the hearing, copies of them and details of variations etc. must be available and details contained in this section.

If the court decides to make a confiscation order the prosecution claim the position is as follows:

Total Benefit	£xxx
Total Realisable Property	£xxx
Possible Confiscation Order	**£xxx**

If the amount that is realisable is less than the benefit then the court should make an order in the lesser sum and fix a default sentence that is set under that amount. If the realisable property is more than the benefit then the benefit figure is the one that should be applied.

Any answer or reply to this statement under Part VI of the Criminal Justice Act 1988 should be addressed to *[name and address of Crown Court]* and a copy sent to the Central Confiscation Bureau at 50, Ludgate Hill, London EC4M 7EX.

Note any advice or assistance on completion of a Prosecutor's Statement should be obtained from the Central Confiscation Bureau.

Signature .... Date ....

Statement tendered by *[name and address of CPS Branch or Confiscation Unit]*.

In all cases where a confiscation order is considered the court may be referred to the case of ONWUKA (1992) which sets out the steps a court may take in such a case.

Appendix III
The Money Laundering Regulations 1993

In total there are 17 Regulations

Regulation 1   Names regulations.

Regulation 2   Interprets meanings of terms such as business relationship and insurance business.

Regulation 3   Defines a business relationship.

Regulation 4   Meaning of relevant and not relevant financial business.

Regulation 5   Systems and training in prevention of money laundering.

Regulation 6   Offences by directors, managers, company secretaries, partners and associates of corporate bodies, partnerships and unincorporated associations.

Regulation 7   Institutes identification procedures.

Regulation 8   Exempts certain postal payments from Regulation 7.

Regulation 9   Identification procedure regarding transactions on behalf of another.

Regulation 10   Identification exemption for certain business covered by other registration.

Regulation 11   Sets out satisfactory identification.

Regulation 12   Record keeping procedures.

Regulation 13   Supplementary record keeping provisions regarding bankrupts and insolvency.

Regulation 14   Internal reporting procedures regarding disclosure.

Regulation 15   List of supervisory bodies.

Regulation 16   Disclosure requirements, list of Appointed Persons/Inspectors

Regulation 17   Transitional provisions regarding past business.

Appendix IV
Section 1 Drug Trafficking Act 1994

PART 1 Confiscation orders
Introductory

1. – In this Act 'drug trafficking' means, subject to subsection (2) below, doing or being concerned in any of the following, whether in England and Wales or elsewhere: *Meaning of 'drug trafficking' and 'drug trafficking offence*

   a) producing or supplying a controlled drug where the production or supply contravenes section 4 (1) of the Misuse of Drugs Act 1971 or a corresponding law;
   b) transporting or storing a controlled drug where possession of the drug contravenes section (1) of the Act or a corresponding law;
   c) importing or exporting a controlled drug where the importation or exportation is prohibited by section 3 (1) of that Act or a corresponding law;
   d) manufacturing or supplying a scheduled substance within the meaning of section 12 of the Criminal Justice (International co-operation) Act 1990 where the manufacture or supply is an offence under that section or would be such an offence if it took place in England and Wales.
   e) using any ship for illicit traffic is controlled drugs in circumstances which amount to the commission of an offence under section 19 of the Act;
   f) conduct which is an offence under section 49 of this Act or which would be such an offence if it took place in England and Wales;
   g) acquiring, having possession of or using property in circumstances which amount to the commission of an offence under section 51 of this Act or which would amount to such an offence if it took place in England and Wales.

2. – 'Drug trafficking' also includes a person doing the following whether in England and Wales or elsewhere, that is to say, entering into or being otherwise concerned in an arrangement whereby:

   a) the retention or control by or on behalf of another person of the other personís proceeds of drug trafficking is facilitated; or
   b) the proceeds of drug trafficking by another person are used to secure that funds are placed at the other personís disposal or are used for the other personís benefit to acquire property by way of investment.

Appendix IV

3. – In this Act 'drug trafficking offence' means any of the following:

   a) an offence under section 4(2) or (3) or 5(3) of the Misuse of Drugs Act 1971 (production supply and possession for supply of controlled drugs);

   b) an offence under section 20 of that Act (assisting in or inducing commission outside United Kingdom of offence punishable under a corresponding law);

   c) an offence under:
      i) section 50(2) or (3) of the Customs and Excise Management Act 1979 (improper importation),
      ii) section 68(2) of that Act (exportation), or
      iii) section 170 of that Act (fraudulent evasion),

      in connection with a prohibition or restriction on importation or exportation having effect by virtue of section 3 of the Misuse of Drugs Act 1971;

   d) an offence under section 12 of the Criminal Justice (International Co-operation) Act 1990 (manufacture or supply of substance specified in Schedule 2 to that Act);

   e) an offence under section 19 of that Act (using ship for illicit traffic in controlled drugs);

   f) an offence under section 49.50 or 51 of this Act or section 14 of the Criminal Justice (International Co-operation) Act 1990 (which makes, in relation to Scotland and Northern Ireland, provision corresponding to section 49 of this Act);

   g) an offence under section 1 of the Criminal Law Act 1977 of conspiracy to commit any of the offences in paragraphs (a) to (f) above;

   h) an offence under section 1 of the Criminal Attempts Act 1981 of attempting to commit any of those offences; and

   i) an offence of inciting another person to commit any of those offences, whether under section 19 of the Misuse of Drugs Act 1971 or at common law;

and includes siding abetting, counselling or procuring the commission of any of the offences in paragraphs (a) to (f) above.

4. – In this section 'corresponding law' has the same meaning as the Misuse of Drugs Act 1971.

5. – For the purposes of the application of Part II of this Act in Scotland Northern Ireland 'drug trafficking' hall be construed in accordance with section 48(2) of this Act.

Index

A - B
British Bankers' Association   27

C
Cash, seizure and detention of   84-6
Central Authority   141-2
Central Drug Authority   143
Charging orders   103-5
    legislation   104-5
    obtaining   103-4
    overview   11
Confiscation
    legislation
       in Northern Ireland   6
       In Scotland   5, 6
       overview   3-4
Confiscation orders   109-27
    compensation   111
    criminal benefit   113
    flow charts   113, 125, 126
    legislation   111-27
    overview   12
    property defined   110-1
Criminal Justice Act 1988
    charging orders   104-5
    confiscation orders   112-4
       assumptions   118-20
       postponement   117
       review   125
    disclosure
       tipping off   36
    money laundering
       defined   21
       specific offences   76-80
    overview   6, 14
    production orders   62-3
    production warrants   68-9
       see also Production orders, sample and Production warrants, sample

prosecutor's statement   121-3
sample   163-5
restraint orders   98-101
tipping off   86-7

D
Disclosure
    legal protection   31
    legislation   32-5
    requirements   29
    terrorism   91-2
    tipping off   35-8
    to police   31-2
Drug monies
    detention   84-6
    seizure   84-6
Drug trafficking
    definition   171-2
    disclosure   32-3, 35-6
    legislation
       overview   5-6
       section 1   171-2
    tipping off   88
    use of   82
       defence   82-3
Drug Trafficking Act 1994
    charging orders   104-5
    confiscation orders   115-7
       assumptions   118, 120-1
       postponement   117-8
       review   126
    disclosure under   32-3
       tipping off   35-6
    forfeiture orders   135
    money laundering
       defined   21
       specific offences   80-3
    overview   5, 13

Index

| production orders | 59-60 |
| production warrants | 65-6 |
see also Production orders, sample and Production warrants, sample
prosecutor's statement	123-4
sample	167-9
restraint orders	97-8
section 1	171-2
seizure and detention of cash	84
tipping off	88

E

European Union	4, 19
Excluded material	54-6
human tissue	55
journalistic material	55-6
personal records	54-5
tissue fluid	55

F - G

Financial Action Task Force (FATF)
20, 140
Financial investigation	
Central Authority	141-2
Central Drug Fund	143
evidence abroad, admissibility of	
	142-3
Letters of Request	141-2
profiling	43
life style booklet	43
overview	7
suspicion	8-9
reasonable grounds	8-9
see also Searches; Social Profiling
Forfeiture orders	131-6
flowcharts	131, 133, 135
Misuse of Drugs Act 1971	133
overview	12
Powers of Criminal	
Courts Act 1973	131
Fraud Trials Committee	6

H - I

| Hodgson Committee Report | 4 |

International Criminal Police	
Organisation (ICPO)	141, 142
International Perspective	139-44
overview	12

L

Legal privilege	52-4
communication	52-3
criminal purpose	53-4
items	53
tipping off	37-8
Letters of Request	141-2

M

Money laundering	
applicant for business	20-1
background	19-20
business relationship	22
evidence of identity	27
corporate responsibility	24
criminal conduct	21-2
defence clause	23
definition	21
disclosure	
identification	
procedures	27-8
legal protection	31
legislation	32-5
requirements	28, 29
tipping off	36
to police	31-2
financial business	
relevant	22
not relevant	23
identification procedures	24-8
account opening	24-5
by post	26
common rule book	24

Index

disclosure,
  requirements of 27-8
  exemptions 27
  postal & telecommunications business 26
  records, retention of 27
  satisfactory identification 24-7
  waiver 27
law enforcement agencies, contact with 27-8
methods 44
  integration 5, 75
  layering 5, 75
  placement or immersion 5, 75
offences of
see Specific offences
overview 4-5, 9-10, 11
penalty 23
prevention
  systems for training 23
searches 41-6
Secretary of State, functions of 30
social profiling 41-6
specific offences of
see Specific offences
supervision
  authorities 28, 3
  inspectors 30-1
  persons 30-1
United Kingdom 19-20
Money Laundering Regulations 1993 20-32, 169
disclosure requirements 29
see also Money laundering

N - O

National Criminal Intelligence Service (NCIS) 19, 28 141
Northern Ireland
  legislation 6, 21, 31

P - Q

Policing
  intelligence-led 7
Prevention of Terrorism (Temporary Provisions) Act 1989
  disclosure under 33, 92
    tipping off 37
  forfeiture orders 136
  money laundering
    defined 21
    specific offences 89-92
  overview 6, 15
  production orders 58-9
  production warrants 64
  restraint orders 101-3
Production orders 49-71
  confidentiality 49-50
  flow chart 57
  legislation 58-63
  overview 11
  PACE 52-6, 60-1
  samples 147-60
  see also Special procedure material; Legal privilege; Excluded material
Production warrants 49-71
  legislation 63-9
  overview 11
  PACE 67
  samples 147-60
  see also Special procedure material; Legal privilege; Excluded material
Prosecutor's statement 121-4
  sample 162-9

R

Restraint orders 95-103
  applications for 95-6
  breach of 96
  legislation 96-103
    Northern Ireland 103
    Scotland 103
  overview 11

Index

S

Scotland
   legislation 5, 6, 21
Searches 41-6
   overview 1
   sensitive material 43
   sources 41-2
   unused material 42
Search warrants
see Production warrants
Securities and Investment Board
   20, 28
Social profiling 41-6
   overview 11
Special procedure material 51-2
Specific offences 21, 75-92
   acquisition 75, 77-8, 82-3
   assisting another 75, 76-7, 81-2
   defences 77, 78, 82-3
   drug trafficking, use of 82-3
   penalties 76, 78, 79, 80-1
   possession 77-8, 82-3
   proceeds
      concealing 75, 79-81
      transferring 75, 79-81
      use of 77-8
Stop and search powers 9
Supervisory authorities 28, 30

T

Terrorism
   assisting 91
      defence 91
      penalty 91
   disclosure 33, 91-2
      defence 92
   financial assistance 89-90
      defence 91
      penalty 91
   funds
      control of 91
      retention of 91
   obtaining contributions 90-1
      defence 90-1
      penalty 91
   overview 6
   tipping off 36-7
Tipping off 86-8
   defence 86
   disclosure 35-8
   offence 86-8
   penalties 87, 88

U

Underground banking 44-6
United Nations 4, 19, 140